The Smiling Forehead
Paradoxes from Dadi to Daughter

Volume 2

Dadi Darshan Dharma

Printed and bound in Canada by Transcontinental, March 2007

© *The Smiling Forehead. Paradoxes from Dadi to Daughter.* Volume II

ISBN: 978-0-9734439-4-3

©2007 Orange Palm Publications
Registration of copyright: first trimester 2007
National Library of Quebec
National Library of Canada

Mailing address: Orange Palm Publications©
235 Rene Levesque Boulevard, Suite 310, Montreal, Quebec, H2X 1N8
Telephone: (514) 255-8700 ~ Facsimile: (514) 255-0478
E-mail: info@palmpublications.com;
Website: http://www.palmpublications.com

Graphic design and illustrations: D.D.D., Lucie Robitaille, Eric Mathieu, and Jocelyne Beaudry
Typesetting: Louise Roy
Book cover: Photo by Simhananda
Jacket cover: Photo by Gaétan A. Brouillard

All rights reserved. No part of this book may be reproduced in any form without permission in writing from the author except to quote, or photocopy specific passages for the purposes of group study.

Publications by Orange Palm Publications:

Buddhas, Bodhisattvas, Khadromas and the Way of the Pilgrim — A Transformative Book of Photography and Pithy Sayings (in three languages). Simhananda. 2007.

Holy-Moly Hiccoughs and Enigmatic Knotty Eructations From the Boffola Belly of Bu'Tai. The Drôleries and Dictums of Crazy Modern Dzog-zen. Ken N.O. Sho. 2007.

Knots of Eternity — Paradoxes from Dadi to Daughter. Volume 1. Dadi Darshan Dharma. 2007.

The Great Golden Garland of Gampopa's Sublime Considerations on the Supreme Path — Contemplative Contemporary Commentaries of Gampopa's Root Text. Volume 1. B. Simhananda 2005.

Paradisal Plums: Peaceful Ponderings from a (Rebel) Pandit's Puce Palm — Aphorisms, Adages, and Analects of Sri Adi Dadi, Volumes 1, 2. Etbonan Karta. 2001.

Forthcoming books:

Flyers from the Boys in the Buddhafield. B. Simhananda.

Paradisal Plums: Peaceful Ponderings from a (Rebel) Pandit's Puce Palm, — Aphorisms, Adages, and Analects of Sri Adi Dadi, Volumes 3, 4. Etbonan Karta.

Publications by Magnificent Magus Publications:

The Divine Concordance of Light III: The Science of Full Moon Invocations from HUMANITY's Heart to HIERARCHY's Will. Etbonan Karta. 2007.

Seven Studies of Soul Stations or Soul-ar Progressions Upon Each of the Seven Cosmic-Physical Rays (an integral excerpt from Collectanea One, *The Divine Concordance of Light*). Etbonan Karta. 2007.

Seven Sacred Stations of the Self & Seven Flaming Fiats of Light Upon the Seven Cosmic-Physical Rays (an integral excerpt from *The Divine Concordance of Light*). Etbonan Karta. 2001.

The Divine Concordance of Light: A Handbook from Heaven to Progression Earth — "The Seven Rays of God: Seven Studies of the Soul's Earthly Pilgrimage of Service Upon the Seven Cosmic-Physical Rays". Etbonan Karta. 2001.

Forthcoming books:

Scriptings of the Soul in Questions of Light. Dadi Darshan Dharma.

The Divine Concordance of Light II: The Science of Invocation and the Art of Affirmation from Station HUMANITY to HIERARCHY's Heart. Etbonan Karta.

Dedication

"To the Enlightened Fool in all of us."

Special Thanks:

Firstly, thank you to Lou for working so closely and devotedly with the author on this special project; thanks also to the dynamic duo of Light-Bulb Luce and Jyoti Joss for the attentive aid given in the great graphic designs and setting of the book's inspired layout; and what can one say about Luce and Jyoti's insightful drawings and inspired illustrations except, "Wow!" Next on the list to be rightly recognized and sincerely thanked is our own Divine Mamma Jo-zee, for her constant encouragement and support of everyone, and for playing the roles of both the eagle-eyed supervisor and mother-hen vis-à-vis the project. And finally, we have Eric the enlightened idea man to thank for the colorful cover design, and our Doc Gaetan for kindly providing for everyone's enjoyment, the inspired front-cover photograph. Thank you to all, visible and invisible, who have helped, or have had an impact upon this book in its various stages of production.

With Blessings and affection,

D.D.D.

Table of Contents

Foreword vii
I.   All the Little Fish 1
II.   Noble Views, Considerations & Wisdoms 15
III.   The Vineyard of the Lord's Business 29
IV.   Speak - Nots 43
V.   The Lion's Love 55
VI.   Then Heaven Happens 69
VII.   Liquid Lava and Love 85
VIII. Beholdings 103
IX.   Dangling Dilemmas 117
X.   Stop! Halt! Whoa! 133
XI.   Sword and Sanctity 149
XII.   Stalwart Sadhakas & Disciplined Disciples 165
Glossary 183

Foreword

The Occidental Master, Dadi Darshan Dharma is a living, laughing buddha of authentic spirituality, and a veritable paradox of the magical verb.

Although a being of great simplicity, his writings reveal to the world a complex wisdom and a spirit of the greatest refinement.

All of the paradoxes and precepts which pepper and enliven this unique book with their light, humor, and surprising depth, act as master keys which can suddenly open doors to many unsuspected aspects of the Truth within-us-all.

Dadi Darshan's pen impels us to question even the most mundane issues in our lives. His thoughts constantly short-circuit our deeply entrenched thought patterns and belief systems. He metaphorically sets the living pages about the Spiritual Path on fire with a desire for the Divine, now.

Dadi dares us to 'be Faultless in fault', to be 'Patient in our impatience', to 'laugh with the tears of the thunderstorm', to be 'jealously un-jealous', to be 'Securely insecure' and to be 'a Saint right down deep into sin'. He mentions off-handedly that "Because you yearned for the Answer, He Handed you the Question", and astutely, he comments that "Because you opened your Eye, He saw Himself".

These paradoxes and precepts are both a wonder and a wake-up call. They mysteriously realign with vigor, seriousness, and fun, our mind's modulations with that of the Spirit's High Vision, (or Dharma View), and they give us a new world-perspective vis-à-vis some immortal truths and common spiritual concepts.

Dadi magically manages to touch our inner Heart in a loving fashion and he Lightly gives the 'Happy Smile' back, once again, to its original owner, the Soul.

May you enjoy this heavenly treasure drove of cosmic chocolate delicacies which are the Paradoxes and Precepts of Dadi as much as I did, and may you 'take time to read it and reflect upon it, even if you don't have time'.

It will not be wasted nor will you regret it.

Yours in Light and Wisdom,

Josée D. Senécal
Chief Editor
Paume de Saint-Germain Publishing Inc.

"In the mean man there is mostly memory, a little Light.
In the advanced man there is no memory, only Light."

D.D.D.

All the Little Fish

I

The Smiling Forehead

Paradoxes from Dadi to Daughter

All the Little Fish

If any bimbo could go boom, and tohubohu blast or beat others without ever being blamed, or brought to the tribunal as a beast, who would there be brazen and bodacious enough to beat back such an obvious incarnation of blackhearted bedevilment?

If any bozo could go boom, and blast, and blight, and bruise and burn others without blame, or without ever being brought to book, could even a bold Bayard, breast such an abominable epiphany of barbaric bewitchment?

If a person could perform perfidy without penalty nor punishment, what pragmatic personality would pose to oppose, such a private appeal to power?

If a personality, blackly-bamboozled, could with bold abandon and bluster, abuse, beguile, and betray any human being without the least bit of attrition, nor retribution, who then would there be to rebuff the ignominy, or resist the blandishment of such a beckoning, yet abominable manifestation of baseness?

If you would truly *renounce* then avoid not the world, but serve it detachedly with an abundance of compassion.

If you would truly *serve* then denounce not the world, but plainly uphold the Open Palm as the hallowed hallmark of *help-without-harm*.

If you could be a wise Heavenly Whale and gulp the whole polluted gulf in one harmless quaff, then grateful and graceful Grace, the Bodhisattva Dolphin, and all the rest of the little fish could finally rest, and simply Be.

If the conscientious sadhaka in disciplinary sadhana could just learn the art of compressing his lips tightly together, whenever his concrete self seeks to converse critically, or to articulate negatively in the mode of censure against brother, or sister, then the Spiritual science of **speaking up** *only when the mouth is completely closed* could become an attainable goal.

If you have gotten anything for free, it has already cost you too much.

If you have gotten something as a gratuity because of Guru Grace, it has already been paid for in full, by Nobody.

If the stalwart sadhaka chooses to speak, he ought to *know* the impact of the Meaning first, and learn all about it after.

If you insist upon giving advice then let it come from the impersonal Heart of the Cosmos, and not from your own poor pulpit of palpitating platitudes and passionate opinions.

If a sadhaka should undertake to travel the planet as a dedicated *world-disciple*, let him presently and resolutely, place *heaven* in the Heart-pocket of his pilgrim shirt; then, let him disinterestedly, place *home* in the right pocket of his pilgrim pants; subsequently, let him (spiritedly) place *hell* in the other, opposite, left pant pocket, the one with a hole in it. Finally, let him, in the taking of every step and before every sitting, tuck-away the 'past' in the unseen 'back hatch' of his pilgrim underpants, as these latter undergo the trek of traipsing along with him *impersonally* upon the planet, yet somehow, always manage to remain unsoiled by the passing panorama of people's pleasure and pain.

If the Master's task is to Teach, then the disciple's duty is to teach himself.

If the Master's task is to transmit the Truth the very instant he perceives there is no sadhaka there to teach, then the sadhaka's duty is to Illuminate both himself and his path, the very instant he realizes there never was a Teacher (there), to transmit the Truth.

If an ordinary machine can effectuate extraordinary things, then the ordinary, mystically-polarized man can surely accomplish *supraextraordinary stuff,* merely by the conscious clicking-off of his *spiritus roboticus.*

Good indeed, it is, to die in God.

Better verily, it is, to Live in the Lord.

If God is what we essentially *are* then Wealth is what we truly *have,* and That... is the Divine Treasure which we are all indebted to *share.*

If Sat, Chit and Ananda are the inherent ABC, (<u>A</u>wareness, <u>B</u>liss, and <u>C</u>onsciousness) of the All-Knowing Brahman... then DEF represents the eternal <u>D</u>harma, <u>E</u>mptiness, and <u>F</u>orgiveness of the all-compassionate Lord Buddha.

If the sadhaka looks a mite too wise, he will surely be made a fool of; but then, of course, a necessary part of Wisdom is also that of looking the fool.

If the sadhaka takes to quibble, quarrel and clash a mite too often, the Master may compassionately quip forth the following clip of contingent counsel:

"Quail the quaking, quarantine the choler, and kill Cain!"

"Quickly!"

If you find GOD first, Virtue will vouch for you later.

If a man be without GOD, then he is a wound without a Heart.

If a woman be without Love, then she is a heart without a Wound.

If you wish to die well yourself, honor respectfully the presently dying, and honor mindfully the process of *deathing* in living.

If you deem to respect SPIRIT, then you must deem hold in esteem the dignity of God **in all men**... whether these men be the good, or the terribly bad; the high, or the servile low; the divine, or the outrageously godless; the loved, or the heinously hated; the saved, or the unfortunately lost.

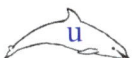

Whether you esteem god, goddess, or devil, know these all as the morbidities, mendacities, and maya of the mind... no matter how Marvelous.

If you have not wit, Wisdom is the poorer. If you have not humor, Holiness is but a (hopeless) heap of humility.

If you truly remember God at all times, you won't ever have to tell the Truth.

If today lacked laughter, it is long lost.

If today skipped a smile, it stays sempiternally sad.

If a disciple desires disinterestedness, let him disengage the suspenders of his self-will.

Let him strip his ego to the bare, and divest himself of the fatigue of narcissism.

Let him go walk awarely awhile, naked as a worm under the moonglow of the Soul's Light.

If only the sadhaka would be bold-spirited and shatter the vase of self-importance, he would return shamefaced to just being, Originally LOVE.

Noble Views, Considerations & Wisdoms

II

The Smiling Forehead

Paradoxes from Dadi to Daughter

Noble Views, Considerations & Wisdoms

Please contemplate the Noble View which says that:

"All of life's bumps and blows; and buntings and bonkings; all of life's bangs and boomerangs, and bongs and bombs; all of life's bare bummers and bucking broncos; all of life's blockbuster blockades and blustering besiegements; all of life's bloody beliefs and boiling blitzkriegs; all of life's bitter boluses and bare, broken bodies; all of life's blights and banes become bearable, even beatifically bovine, in our Basic BEING's Remembrance."

Resumé:

All of life's blights and banes become bearable, (even bovine), in Holy Remembrance.

Please ponder the universal perspective which unblinkingly reveals that:

"Unhappiness is part of the personality; and the ego has (multiple) shares in its stock."

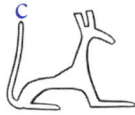

Please contemplate the Noble View which percipiently reflects that:

"It is painful to be with people of polluted mind where self-will rules and anger rages, where passions imprison and envy empoisons, where mirages abound and illusions prosper."

"Only in the taking of persistent and present Refuge in the DIVINE NAME, will the disciple perfectly protect his (inner and outer) person; and permute a Spiritual Knowing and a Subtle Refinement into the detailed destiny of his daily life."

Perfectly ponder the provocative perspective that:

GOD *Mantras forth His Name into all space at all times, within and without.*

"How then, can you possibly be without Him unless your ear is unhearingly tuned to your narcissistic self, as you eagerly endeavor to repeat the mantra of the living moment, egoically?"

Please contemplate the Noble View, playfully musing that:

"No one's oral orifice can expand wide enough to broadcast the whole Truth."

"No mandibles can open wide enough to form the perfect OM."

"No broad massive yawn can be bored enough to eclipse the Wonder of the world."

Please ponder upon the ensuing thought perspective:

"Behold everyone is of God and everyone is Chosen."

"If you Behold other than this you are beholden to, and are beholding, a bold untruth."

Please contemplate the Noble View venerating that:

"A Buddha's body is a joss-burner of Heavenly aromatic Light."

"A Buddha's breath is a sweet-scented bouquet of Dharma Blessings."

Perfectly ponder the spiritual perspective which says that:

"The sweat of a Buddha is attar from afar and it is secreted from the core of a Spiritual Star."

Please contemplate the Noble View acknowledging that:

"No bindings can oblige the Absolute; no borders can befringe the Boundless."

Perfectly ponder the intriguing vista that:

"You perceive parts and partiality because of a partitioned Mind and a partial Perspective."

"You see splinterings and separations because of a segmented Sight and a scattered Vision."

Please contemplate the Noble View which professes that:

"God is the Alpha-point of Creation; Man is the Omega-point of the Manifest."

"God-as-Man and Man-as-God make up One inseparable, indispensable, Unity of Mind."

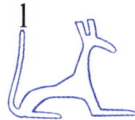

Please incline your mind to the blissful prospect which states that:

"The Lord has become the Beloved of all Lovers, for such a Boundless, All-Embracing Lover Is He."

Please contemplate the Noble View which sapiently avers that:

"God is crazy-glued to you, yet He never *contacts* you, other than by His unconditional encompassing of the All of Creation."

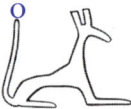

In awakening to Wisdom,

"Know that all misfortune, mishap, and misunderstanding immediately melts into a milky mirkiness of magenta marsh-mellowness; or else, mysteriously mutates to a mousy mauve mousse through the Mindful minding of 'Magna Mater'."

Being Wise, arise, and

"Stop, stop, stop!"

Stop pushing the impertinent pencil of personal power, and thenceforth, reap the response of a Self-pertinent Patience.

In penetrating to Sagacity,

"Promote prema, prema, prema, and pray that Purusha not forget to program into your Life Plan, the indefinite pauses of indispensible, Spiritual Want."

In awakening to Wisdom,

"Do Dharma, kill karma!"

Delight in Dharma, be kind to your karma, and die in Yamantaka.

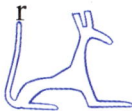

Being wise, arise, and

"Touch to the Truth within and tote it Tranquilly, (without)."

In penetrating to Sagacity,

"Do not finger yourself as unfit if feeling enfeebled; you may just be one of the few, whose self-defences have (finally) failed."

Fetch up Faith, rather, and cast forth your helplessness upon the waters of the Spirit.

Fetch up Faith, rather, and let yourself be carried forthwith upon the bosom of the MOTHER's Oceanic Love.

In awakening to Wisdom,

"Act like a Spiritual Snail, and make of your body a moving Mandir of Mahanam, and let the whole world become your Ashram in motion."

Being Wise, arise, and

"Know Divine Diksha as a Real Revelation, sinking somewhere deep within the Mind and Heart; and regard it not as some sort of spiritually-sorry outer initiation, with some sort of miracle mantra, secretly attached to the Blessing."

In penetrating to Sagacity,

"Realize that the sadhaka does not gallop after the Guru; he sharp-shoots for the Self."

In awakening to Wisdom,

"Know that no man can order Life; but all men can put their lives in order."

Being wise, arise, and

"Let all whining become widowed and unwholesome worry wither; let Ishwara-within become a window and Lord Kwannon be your Wisdom."

Let war withdraw and wrong-willfulness wilt, and let Woden be your wizard and Wyrd your wind.

In penetrating to Sagacity,

"Waste not His Love and want not other than His Will."

In awakening to Wisdom,

"Could it be your Teacher who is a (controlling) tyrant; or is it you, who are a defiant and disrespectful disciple?"

"Could it be your Master who is wrong, (and in grave error); or is it you, who are a blind and dumb disciple?"

"Could it be your Guru who is a pretender, and truly false; or is it you, who are (really) an unfaithful and fraudulent disciple?"

"Could it be your Instructor who is a manipulator and is (unreasonably) demanding; or is it you, who are really an undisciplined and unheedful disciple?"

"Could it be your Guide who is indifferent, (and non-caring); or is it you, who are a diffidently-dependent disciple, and a please-pay-attention-to-me, self-absorbed sadhaka?"

"Could it be your Sheik who is exploitive and spiritually-selfish, (and even ambitious); or is it you, who are an aspiring sishya, full of self-solicitude, self-satisfaction and self-seeking?"

"Could it be your Roshi who is inconsiderate, unvirtuous, and what's more, of superficial Illumination; or is it you, who is really (still) a disciple of unprepared Spirit and of insufficient Cultivation?"

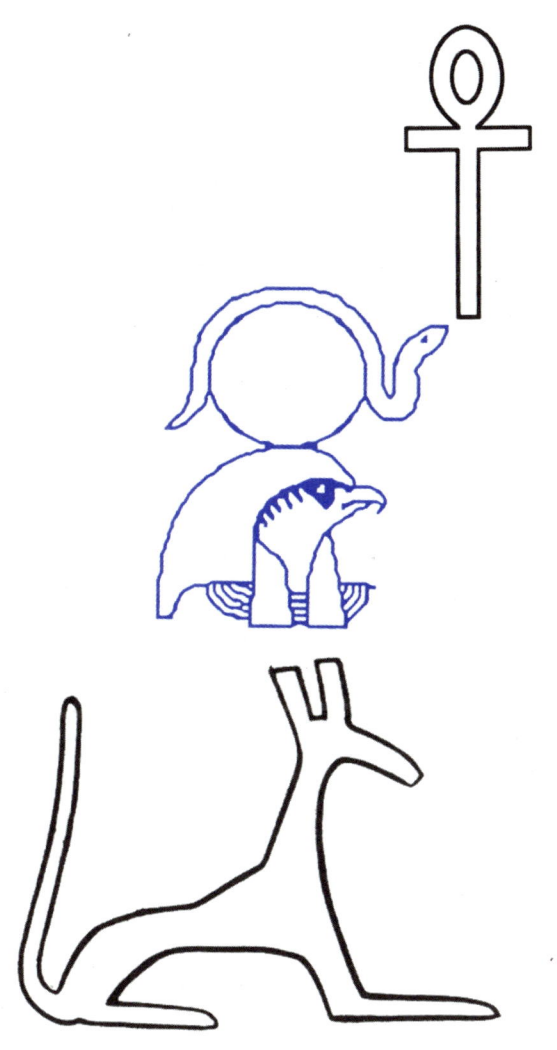

The Vineyard of the Lord's Business

III

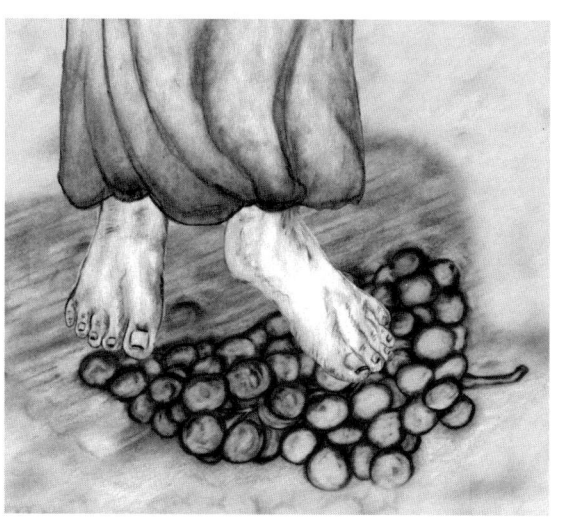

The Smiling Forehead
Paradoxes from Dadi to Daughter

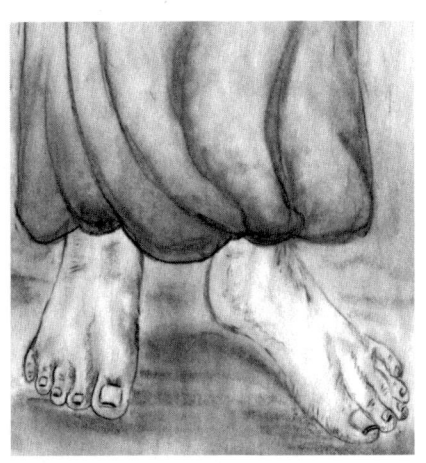

The Vineyard of the Lord's Business

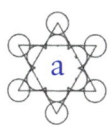

Your Brother, the enemy, perniciously promises to push, pull, persecute, and pleasure you to Spiritual perdition.

(If perchance, he is not able to make much headway with such devious tactics, he will simply opt to take you to task by selfishly taking up as much of your time as possible, in order to make you lose out, in Divinely-devoted time and Spiritual accomplishment.)

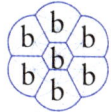

Even if everyone is free to choose, to opt for evil is to cease to be free.

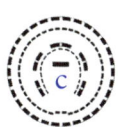

SPIRIT presses upon a sadhaka's consciousness like upon grapes for the making of Wine.

(But never would SPIRIT presume to **oppress** the sadhaka's Spirit for the least purpose of Quality Vintage.)

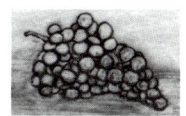

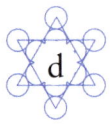

No matter how Spiritually deaf and blind a disciple has sadly become, whether it is through an *astral mirage*, or a projected *personal glamour*; or whether it is through plain pride, ambiguous ambition, or a stubborn self-will ... it still remains within the domain of the Law of Vibration that a contemplated, deliberated, planned, or even reactionary wrong choice, wrong action, or wrong direction undertaken upon the Path, *clangs* the sadhaka's Consciousness cacophonously with the Inner Alarm of the Soul's S.O.S... and this, no matter how comfortably liberating, obviously righteous, or politically correct a sequence of action, or system of philosophy, may seem to be.

(The Soul will continue to vibrate forth Its unease until the Holy Spirit's intended message **of** *Spiritual Error*, is clearly heard by the sadhaka's wayward mind, even *after Death itself* has tolled its bell.)

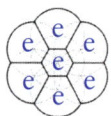

Spirit gives the *common man* ample space to make mistakes... *over and over again.*
(It's part and parcel of the false freedom.)

Spirit gives a *sadhaka* the simulated space to make mistakes... *only once.*

Spirit gives an *initiate* the nonsubsistent space to make mistakes... *at his Spiritual Peril.*

The showering of Grace imposts an imperative of *augmented Answerability*.

The tonsure of Sonship imposes an urgency of *aggravated Responsibility*.

When I abide in SPIRIT, I appear less, yet Am everywhere, more.

When I abide in God, I am no more; yet, the whole of Creation exalts in me.

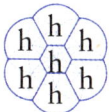

The Saint looks upon a person's heart as if God is compassionately taking note.

Better to be a mere lamb of the Lord than a magnanimous magnate of the world.

Oh better still to be both! A child of God and a selfless server of the World!

Oh better still, just to Be, or not to Be; or to Be this, or to Be that... as the Lord Wills, AHA!

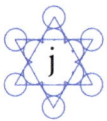

To the stalwart and steadfast sadhaka, each daily duty, *(especially the most mundane)*, comes straight from the Boss and takes place in the Vineyard of the Lord's Business.

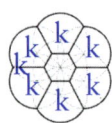

When the sadhaka shamelessly shirks *tyaga,* he undergoes *tapasya* tactlessly, without the reckoning, nor blessings, of the sagacious Naga King, who is also the stately steward of the ascetic Lord SHIVA.

The Sun shines all day; the Moon shines all night: it is their divine duty to Shine.

Are you as SOUL shining day and night, all the while, in Divine Duty to the SELF?

Things are to be Lovingly used; people are to be lovingly Loved.

Disciples are to be Lovingly *used*; Initiates are to be Lovingly *abused.*

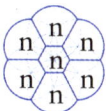

The moving moment is gone in an instant and fades immediately into the mirage of memory.

Hello, was anybody really there?

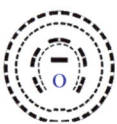

Pity for those who, for some superficial paltry pleasure, dispense themselves of their Divine dignity, and who sadly, for the sake of a fast forgotten fling, heedlessly throw off, (in a mounting moment of desire), their avowed Discipleship.

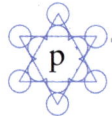

Brotherhood recognizes in every man, a Soul's acknowledged worth.

Brotherhood awakens in every receptive man, a sense of Spiritual Sonship.

Brotherhood testifies to the dignity of the Divine in every man and woman, without consideration of color, creed, or country.

Brotherhood (unconditionally) Cares, because all human sons and daughters are born of God, are borne by God, and are brought (back) to God, through His One Love for all.

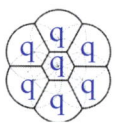

The raggedy rags of the rich but 'poor in Spirit', as well as the cast-off cloth of those who have sadly denuded themselves of God, must of necessity have a Master Tailor to teach them the craft of weaving the Sacred Thread back into the weft and woof of their lonely Lives.

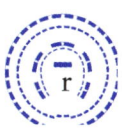

Have you been basely betrayed, lately?
Have you been woefully wronged, all along?
Have you been wolfishly wounded, and awfully so?

Have you a pain that is poignant and (dreadfully) deep?

Consider the following Acrid Cupful:
>'What toll the anger?'
>'What price the resentment?'
>'What cost the bitterness?'
>'What waste the playbacks?'
>'What calamity the payback?'
>'What karma the (killing) hate?'

Judicious by far to forbear, and to forgive; superior by far to spare, and to pardon.

To ply self to the Father's Will is the quintessence of Obedience.

To share joyfully in the Father's Will is the highest of Honors.

To realize, vivifyingly, the Father's Will is by far, the greatest of Accomplishments.

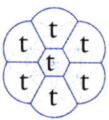

AN ASPIRANT'S PRAYER:

"Help me, O Lord, to accept more in life than I can (cynically) criticize.

Help me, O Lord, to give more to life than I can (personally) receive.

Help me, O Lord, to intromit more into life than I can (possibly) extirpate.

Help me, O Lord, to proffer and uphold more of life than I can *ignorantly* waste, or *ignominiously* condemn."

Grant me, O Lord, the Soul's gift of Grafting God into the very fabric of LIFE's multifold Plan.

For the true and tried Disciple, Divine Detachment involves first of all, the capacity to discern accurately the Will of the Father; and secondly, the ability, the strength and the steadfastness to follow That Will, no matter what transpires in the personal life.

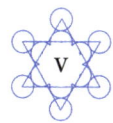

A Disciple's Privilege:

"In my having Remembered Thy Name unceasingly, O Lord, permit me presently, to awaken in the sleep of Thy Princely Peace.

In my having devotedly Served Thy Truth always, O Lord, permit me presently to take action in the exaltation of Thy Illumined Will.

In my having faithfully Loved Thy Light infinitely, O Lord, permit me presently to bathe in the bliss of Thy Effulgent Sight.

In my having practised steadfastly Thy Presence, O Lord, permit me presently, to rest in the ever-present Reality of Thy Eternity."

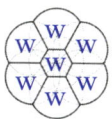

Are you a man of mouth, a man of deed, or a man of Being?
Are you a man of gab, a man of gizmos, or a man of God?

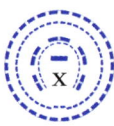

Are you a man of sensation, a man of emotion, or a man of Heart?
Are you a man of matter, a man of mind, or a man of Life?

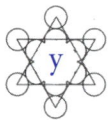

Are you an outer man, an inner man, or a Spiritual man?
Are you a material man, a mantric man, or a Monadic man?

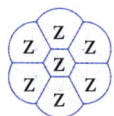

The finite flesh is the frail fiery form of the Father's Flame.

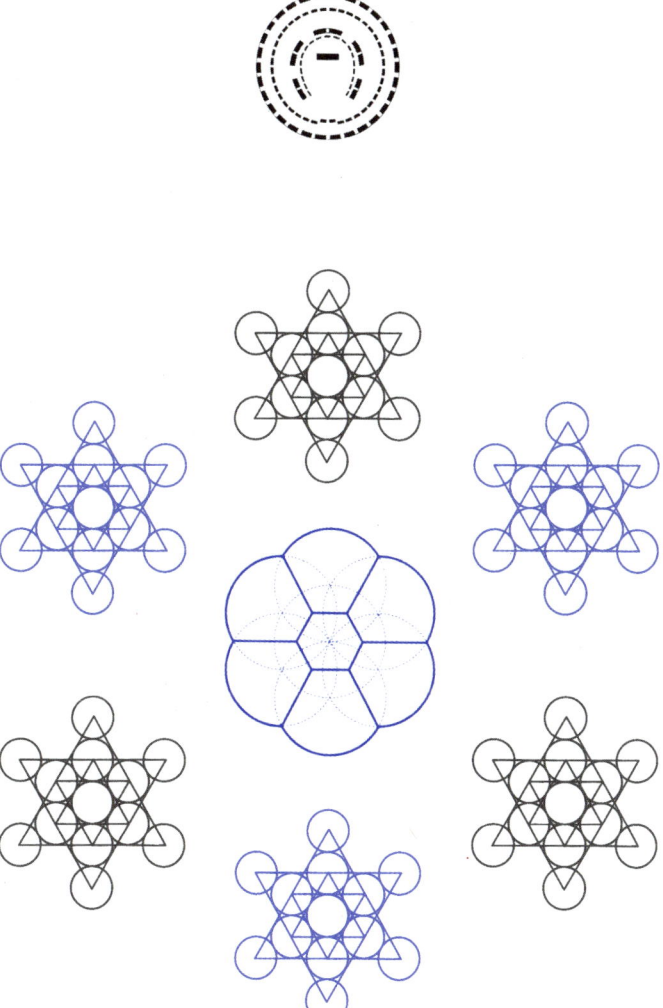

Speak - Nots

IV

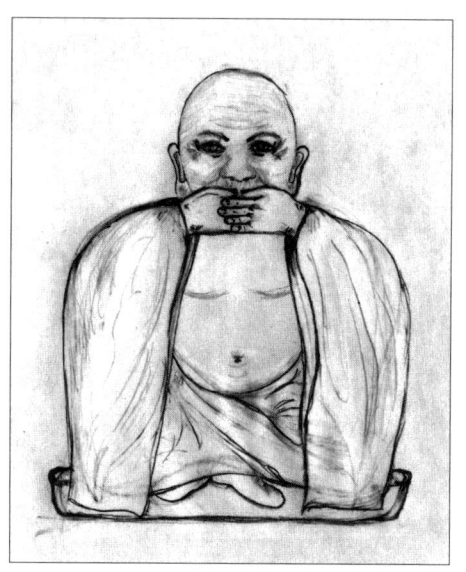

The Smiling Forehead
Paradoxes from Dadi to Daughter

Speak - Nots

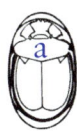

Speak not, O sadhaka, of Pharisees and Philistines from the superior platform of the Path, until:

>   all of your (projected) pains have been properly poulticed;

>   all of your (private) punctures have been Spiritually-penicillined;

>   all of your (personal) piety, piousness, and pontifications have been uprooted;

>   all of your (unperceived) hypocrisies have been apprehended, and upended.

These healings, of course, can only come to pass through the pure *krupa* and Godspeed-power of the Master's applied 'Spiritual Pharmacopoeia'.

Speak not ill of any being. *It weakens the self.*
Speak not critically of another. *It accuses the self.*
Speak not contemptuously of anyone. *It condemns the self.*

Speak not of the Impersonal, until the self and all that is personal, has profoundly prostrated before Purusha.

Speak not of righteous Justice unless the (whole) Truth has been brought to Light.

Speak not any word upon which God cannot disembark.

Speak not of SUSPICION... unless you yourself are above that.

It is never good work to infer a snap guilty verdict, especially when the case is thin and the proof is poor, and the impulse is perhaps one of hurt pride, or wounded vanity.

Speak not of Enlightenment until you have become the Lord's Light... illuminating always Innocently the PATH, through your (humble) *body-bundle* of Bliss.

Speak not of Surrender until you have delivered yourself to Him, and all self-defence, (*cough, cough*), has definitely died.

Speak not of Existence until you have *ceased to exist*... (that is), until the small self has scrubbed itself out into Pure Remembrance.

Speak not of Fullness until you have absented into the Void, that is, until the little 'I' has fallen *irretrievably* forgotten, into great Goddess MAHAKALI's magnificent, devouring maw.

Speak not of the Guru as if he is the Way... the Way is to get Lost, and never quite find, your way back again.

Speak not of real strength until humility itself has deeply-bowed to the Self.

Speak not of true power until Wisdom has been empowered by the skillful transmission (to you) of your Teacher's Will.

Speak not of Absoluteness until all of your activity harmlessly expresses just 'Isness'.

Speak not of Nothingness until all of your actions transmute openly into just 'Beingness'.

Speak not of the Truth until all effort to tell It has failed.

Speak not of the Lord without your burning desire for Him, ravaging all ground before you.

Speak not of '*Nondualism*' without having ditched the dual bind of a (dichotomous) Mind and the duality of (a divided) Divinity.

Speak not of RAMA without knowing Him to be SITA.

Speak not of relevant Reality without essential Unity.

Speak not of the Word without having excised all language.
Speak not of the Verb without having wiped-out all words.

Speak not of personal Realization without impersonal Revelation.

Speak not of True Love without Real Crucifixion.

Speak not of Resplendent Beauty without Godly Presence; and speak not of Effulgent Emptiness without the Buddha's Radiance.

Speak not of Divine Fragrance without the Scent of the Soul.

Speak not of Crowning Grace without Master Accomplishment.

Speak not of Infinite Mystery without the Transcendental Mind.

Speak not of Mary's Mercy without CHRIST, the Son of COMPASSION.

Speak not of the Goddess KWAN YIN's omnipresent Compassion, without simultaneously acknowledging the Illumined Bodhicitta, and Universal Pathos of Her Brother... the Blessed Lord, AVALOKITESWARA.

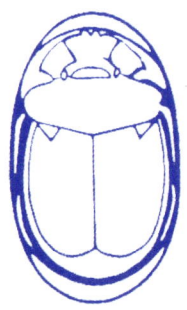

The Lion's Love

V

The Smiling Forehead

Paradoxes from Dadi to Daughter

The Lion's Love

Since neither you nor I exist, *Love only Him*, in not-you and not-me.

Because you are a priori, a personal-impersonal part and parcel of the Planetary Potentate, wise therefore, it would be to presently *pranaam* and do private *puja* to your (own) Poor Emperor.

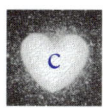

Because LOVE is All-Merciful know that you already have Mary's MERCY.

Therefore, be of good cheer and merry-be-Mary, on your Merciful Way.

The Lion's Love

Because you decidedly delivered all desire and doings to the Divine, the unspeakable Pod of Purple Peace did plummet deeply into your already wounded Heart.

And thusly Wounded, you can now *impeccably pray* for the planet.

Because the whole world is already always wedded to God, does not the very next heartbeat present you with an auspicious opportunity for some Unio Mystica?

Because man tends restlessly to seek God, he usually fails to find Him.

Instead, let him take to the Good, the True and the Beautiful, and in so doing, become God-like.

Thusly, and only thereafter, can there be a DIVINE RECOGNITION of some significant, Spiritual sorts.

Since pain and pleasure and everything in between is a selfless gift from God, what can one do but to acquiesce, and say, "Yes, Sri Devi", with a tranquil equanimity and a fierce Love.

Because you did not heed God-in-other, you are indeedy, in Divine debt.

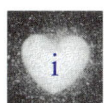

Because the Esoteric (No-) NAME is the hidden and pulsing Y-factor of the Manifest Game, you must respect and protect the Exoteric (Good) Name, of each and every manchild of God.

Since the senses sensate they can truly *sense* God.

(In their essential nature, they have a *sensational* right to Him; therefore, do not cause some senseless separation in your self, by *senselessly* starving the Sensei of the senses to death.)

Because karma is already a done doing, a future 'Divine Doing' is, of course, the only possible doorway out of the karmic labyrinth.

Since your left hand is held by Him assuredly, your right hand can now do its daily dharma, devotedly.

Because time is precious, preciously precious indeed, is a prompt pardon.

Because world discipleship is Divine, the beneficent disciple should ever be without dread when dealing in Divinity, for the sake of sentient man.

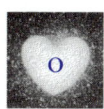

Because you have forgotten yourself, *fear* has forever fled your doorstep.

Because you have no fear presently, a *fragrance* preambulates your footstep.

Because you have now a Fragrance, *essence* flows from your very Soul.

Because you have now become a flowing Essence, each footfall is finally, set Free.

Because too much money is found in too few hands, inharmonious harm is done to parity and happiness flees the world.

Too much money which has agglutinated gluttonously in some cheering section of the material world may please **Dr. Mara** at the **Maya Clinic**, but in passing time, its tremulous and tumorous merit is found to be most always, deadly *malignant*.

Too much of anything in any one place is anathema to the equitable allotment and equipotent apportionment of the universal essence of Spirit being transformed into shared Substance.

Because of Life, Love listened, and I learned how to *love*.

Because of Love, Life listened, and I learned how to *live*.

Because of the pervasive poverty of spiritual speech on the planet, there has piled up omnipresently, a pervading penury of Divine deed.

Because evil scratches in the dank and dark to evoke fear, the disciple must steadfastly invoke his daily armor of Light, with a ready spirit and a disciplined Love.

On the other hand, the Initiate instantly dispels the dark with his Light and never gets to know fear, because of the spontaneous Love ever rising within the spaciosity of his BEING.

Because BEAUTY was imbued with Bodhi, the Buddha bore Her brightly into His Breast and bade Her bear lightly His burden of Benign Bodhicitta.

Because you broke the bones of your burdensome bodies upon the Anvil of BRAHMAN, you broke through to the Bonified BRIGHT, and shattered your unsheltered Self into some ten thousand splintered pieces of absolute, Beatific Bankruptcy.

Because you deem yourself as being ready to risk all for God, He will most certainly take you to serious test, but so will the Devil's own.

Because you done surrendered your sins to the Savior, He tenderly took care of your Re-hab, and dauntlessly subsidized your Discipleship-Tab.

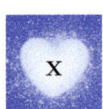

Since this *here* second is *now* history-ing 'YOU' forth as your SELF's *Impeccable Intent*, be Aware, be Here, be Now... for you won't get a *second* chance!

Since Spiritually-speaking, nothing happens which is mere happenstance, the seemingly circumstantial situations and events, the accidents, or the near-accidents that we undergo, have all been Intelligently set-up by the SOUL.

The Soul masterfully shapes substance and lesson, energy and economy, consciousness and expansion into a much greater jivatmic *Awaring* of the great interconnectedness and fundamental closeness of all dimensions of Being and Doing.

Since we who are still alive have survived the tests and trials of Life, we have also, certainly derived many a hard-earned lessons from all of the diverse situations spun-out and spirited-forth to the physical plane, by the Inspired Intent of the SELF.

Indeed, how Spiritually-salutary and indubitably Blessed are all our adventures and misadventures, (gross or subtle), which we have had to undergo on our inexorable way toward an ever-more conscious, *evolutionary*, (non-accidental), Freedom.

Since the Lion's LOVE is Perfectly Pure, It Compassionately hunts down all impure prey, and kills them with a perfect Mind.

Then Heaven Happens

VI

The Smiling Forehead

Paradoxes from Dadi to Daughter

Then Heaven Happens

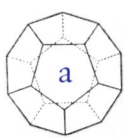

The Guru Himself has no Grace... he simply *breathes to bequeath Baraka*... in spontaneously poetic portions of constant Giving.

The AUM-opened sadhaka who has orbited the Original Face has now the overwhelming obligation of occultly obeying the ONE as being Omnipotently OM, Omnisciently AH, and Omnipresently HUM.

Real prayer when *praying* truly, never thirsts; real love when *loving* truly, never hungers.

Then Heaven Happens

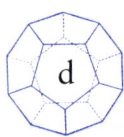

The whole wide world may be laid to waste and wash away, but the worthy disciple who has learned to walk over the waters of apparent chaos and woe, takes up a wide-awake and instantaneous watch, and patiently waits like a wise wizard, meditatively poised upon a Promontory of Peace.

The Glory of the Cross is my decreed death; the folly of the Cross is my forlorn, (already) forgotten life.

The saintly Sufi selflessly shares the suffering of the selfish serf.

The saintly Sheik selflessly shares the suffering of the selfish sufi.

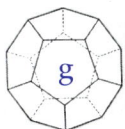

The time that you spend in dissension is lost to Loving.

The time that you spend in faultfinding is lost to Kindness.

The time that you spend in self-justification is lost to right-Mindfulness.

The time that you spend in self-significance is lost to the Empty Self.

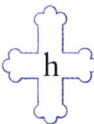

The sadhaka who seriously sets about his sadhana, seriously gets to Shine in secreted sheets of Godly-Gold.

The indeflectable karma of kismet kama quickly kindles the uncontrolled kiss of two kindred egocentricities into an echolalic incandescence of crackling passion, sweetly-skippered by the love-crazed and ecstatic, Capitan Cupid.

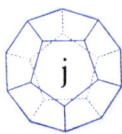

Ponder perfectly upon Padmakara and you peregrinate in Peace.

Proffer a perpetual prayer to Padmapani and you perdure in Peace.

Prophesize, psalmize and poetize the Perfect One, and you proliferate a powerful, pleasurable Peace from pole to pole upon the planet.

Plead, propitiate, and prevail at all times in the Prajnaparamitas, and you prostrate forth omnipotently a deep Dispassionate Peace at all key points of the compass.

The concrete cogitator and its contracted corpus of convoluted Conceptual Call are crooning, conniving cohorts, who are constantly concocting up a crooked core-commerce of cupidity and concupiscence in the candid Consciousness.

Monadic Memorandum:

Take note that the nescient obscuration of the occultly Real is cluelessly accomplished in circuitous contraposition to the conscious composition of the correct, metamorphic consecration of the personal psyche to the Seraphically Sacred.

The probationer is 40% (laid-back) sadhana and 60% aspiration.
The disciple is 40% spiritual service and 60% self-deception.
The initiate is 40% clear wisdom and 60% divine bullshit.

The Guru is 40% godly gruff and 60% cream-puff.

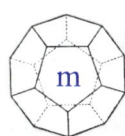

There is no Light cut-off from the DIVINE CLAP.
There is no Love uncoupled from the SELF.
There is no Liberty freed from SERVICE.
There is no Truth sectioned off from REALITY.
There is no Passion unfettered from HEAT.
There is no Life divorced from LIFE.

There is no Soul separate from the SELF.
There is no Self sundered from EMPTINESS.
There is no Spirit split from the ABSOLUTE VOID.

Real Religion is closely related to the Natural Respiration of the Inner Being blissfully breathing forth (Its) Essential Emptiness.

Love comes from the CENTRAL CORE.
Light comes from RADIANT EMPTINESS.
Liberty comes from TRUTH.
Liberation comes from FREEDOM.

Lila comes from RE-CREATION.

Ties come from TIME.
Relationship comes from ATTRACTION.
Bondage comes from ATTACHMENT.
Suffering comes from IDENTIFICATION.

Existence comes from SPACE.

Blindness comes from SIGHT.
Hearing comes from SILENCE.
Touching comes from SOLITARINESS.
Aloneness comes from INITIATION.

Beingness comes from NAUGHT.

Creation comes from (DIVINE) DESIRE.
Soulness comes from SELF.
Birth comes from SACRIFICE.
Death comes from LIFE.

God comes from the HU-MAN.
Life comes from the Vast Void of (the) spontaneous ALL-ARISING.

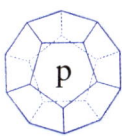

The Lord cannot Live without LIFE lifting Him high, as the All That Is Beyond the BEYOND, and Higher than (the) HIGHEST.

Disciples dare not divorce Divinity from the daily doing of Dharma.

Even as people speak pro you, or against you, it remains in the main your daily Dharma duty to practice generating peace, and making whoopee with your own Soul-appropriated tasks, trials and tests, and all Self-dispensed *prarabdha karma* reapings.

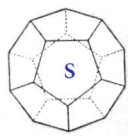

I am not a Saint, a Sheik, nor a Saddhu.

I am not a Yogi, a Guru, a Master, a Rinpoche, a Lama (Lord), nor an Avatara.

In Truth, only a Lord Maitreya, a Lord Manjushri, a Maha-Avatara (like BABA-ji), or a Sri Satya Sai, can be any, or all of these.

I am only Mind Beyond mind.

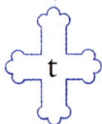

Overall, the all of it matters very little at all... but mysteriously, it is all important.

A Master does not make a miracle.

He Divinely aims at Naught and then Heaven Happens, once upon a helpless happenstance, somewhere on earth.

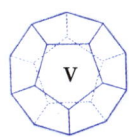

Overwork overestimates your force and overdraws your basic vitality.

Overexertion overhauls you overwrought and overdue into overtime.

Overindulgence overdrives the dualistic, desire-based senses, and overtakes your prana.

Overimportance overspends the self and overdoes one's pride.

Oversexuality overtaxes your ovaries and overheats your oven.

Overstimulation overshoots your ovae and overdrains your oojas.

Overabundance overawes the overneedy. Oversharing overestimates an overflow of oversupply.

Overbuying overlays an overobvious overbalance. Overratedness overesteems an oversense of oversufficiency.

Oversize opinions overstuff your overcoat, and overload your overalls.

Overknowingness overshadows your overlook, and overwhelms your Overview.

Overtrustfulness is overinnocence. Overcredibility is overnaivety. Overopenness is overdangerous.

Overtalking overrides your Overseer. Oversensitivity overclouds your Oversoul.

Overreligiosity overrules your Overmaster. Overreligiousness overthrows your Overlord.

Overpowerfulness is overcompensation. Overenterprise is overambition. Overcontrol is overonericity.

Overempowerment overtly overpushes, oversteps, and overrides the overweak, the overpoor, the overmystical and the oversensitive, for overlong.

A real Realizer does not know anything; he Is everything, known and unknown.

To the wise Wali, water and wine wage no war; both are winsome winners and both waltz wonderfully within the Wholeness of God.

Yet, since time immemorial, water and wine have warred and have been both wild and wicked. On the other hand, water and wine have been totally wholesome and well-wishing too, in warmly and wholeheartedly welcoming the worn and weary wayfarer.

Water and wine have brought whirlwinds of worry and wound, of waste and woe everywhere; yet, water and wine have always been worldly and otherworldly worshipped, and have wrought wreaths of well-being upon all those who have worked willingly upon their willful wills.

Water and wine have waylayed, weakened and withered many a noteworthy warrior upon the Walkway; yet, water and wine have ever been and ever will be, the silent, wild witnesses to a man's Worth.

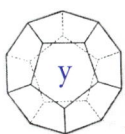

Heaven's Call first checks out as the HEART-ache within all things.

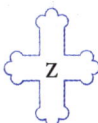

In contraposition to your continuing suffering and to your remembering, (forgiving and forgetting), all that has been said, thought and done *against* you, spare no effort to take note of the following spiritual missive:

It was all part of your Soul's plan. It was all part of your Self's purpose. It was all part of your Destiny's perfect pattern.

The all of it Impelled you forward toward the attainment of a permanent and perfect realisation of the PARAM PARAM PURUSHA, upon your personal planet of painful, *private progression*.

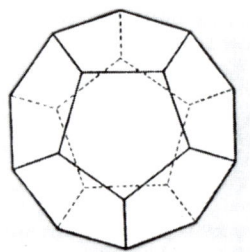

Liquid Lava and Love

VII

The Smiling Forehead
Paradoxes from Dadi to Daughter

Liquid Lava and Love

a

The Essence of Spirit naturally ecstacizes even over a delectable mouthful of barley soup, minus the muscular beef.

The great hunger for God is not about some spiffy vegetarian, (almost mystical) menu, nor about some nifty divine diet, emphasizing a sattvic regime.

The Elevator to God shoots esoterically right by, or right through, all restaurant towers and nutty, nutritional conventions.

b

Dare to discover your own intimate Intuitive Truth, and consider it as futile and sterile, to dare *data-base* Its essential Emptiness to others.

c

In those desperate and discouraging moments when it seems that you just cannot do anything of what it is that you should, or must do at all costs, it may be of a wiser order to practice assiduously the spiritual art of simply letting yourself be saved by the Sweet Isness and Radical Emptiness of things, as they stand.

Liquid Lava and Love

To contemplate the passing moment purely is *to be pregnant with Emptiness.*

To awaken Bodhicitta intelligently is *to give birth to the sweet essence of Compassion.*

To celebrate the spontaneously arising, dualistically-concocted Creation in spacious correctness, is to naturally enjoy the All- of-It whole-heartedly; and yet, in spite of the wholesome Joy, one must stay in a sapient stability of Being throughout the entire process of the *identification of oneself with the inherent Nature of Naught.*

The POSTULANT perceives other and sees *two.*
The DISCIPLE perceives other and sees *two upon-a-point.*
The INITIATE perceives other and sees *the Self alone.*
The MASTER perceives other and sees *No One.*

The Crazy Wisdom Guru, however, secretly sees TAT *beating* TVAM *upon the* ASI, *with a passionate Agape and a wild, uproarious Godly glee.*

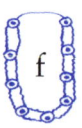

Pursue your *psyche*, not your peers; pursue your *spirit*, not your stars.

The Nullifying Effects and Voiding Affects of Fear

1. POWER commandeered by fear lapses into *corruption,* but more often than not, into subtle, (or outright), *tyranny.*

2. STRENGTH seared by fear lapses into *powerlessness,* but more often, into *heroic fantasy.*

3. TRUTH tarnished by fear lapses into *falsity.*

4. LOVE lanced by fear lapses into *falseheartedness.*

5. WISDOM faulted by fear lapses into *crystallized clarity,* frozen *vision,* or subtle *folly.*

6. BEAUTY besoiled by fear lapses into *seductiveness.*

7. REALITY warped by fear lapses into *coverup.*

8. ILLUMINATION infringed upon by fear lapses into *illusion.*

9. ENLIGHTENMENT empoisoned by fear lapses into *delusion.*

10. UNICITY undercut by fear lapses into *two-facity.*

11. AUTHENTICITY adumbrated by fear lapses into *pharisee-ism.*

12. GOODNESS goaded by fear metamorphoses into *do-goodiness.*

13. LUCIFER disfigured by fear metamorphoses into *darkness.*

14. KARMA accentuated by fear metamorphoses into *cacophonichaosity.*

15. DEVOTION despoiled by fear metamorphoses into *blindness.*

16. SPIRITUALITY stigmatized by fear metamorphoses into *sanctimony*.

17. SADHANA saddled by fear metamorphoses into ritual *fixity*.

18. SERVICE speared by fear metamorphoses into *meritoriousness*.

19. SACRIFICE shackled by fear metamorphoses into subtle *selfishness*.

20. DISCIPLINE dogged by fear metamorphoses into *rigidity*.

21. DISCIPLESHIP desecrated by fear metamorphoses into a *Judas*.

22. MASTERSHIP mantled by fear metamorphoses into *ignominy*.

23. FACT shakened by fear crashes into *factitiousness*.

24. ACTIVITY contaminated by fear crashes into *misdoing*.

25. CERTAINTY crippled by fear crashes into *doubt*.

26. FAITH pilfered by fear crashes into *cynicism*.

27. TRUST tarnished by fear crashes into *treason*.

28. FIDELITY penetrated by fear crashes into *infidelity*.

29. VIRTUE violated by fear crashes into *morality*.

30. UNDERSTANDING undermined by fear crashes into *misapprehension*.

31. COMPASSION cursed by fear crashes into hollow *empathy*.

32. COURAGE casketed by fear crashes into *cowardice*.

33. VIGILANCE validated by fear crashes into *heedlessness*.

34. CRITICALNESS scarred by fear catabolizes into *contempt*.
35. JUDGEMENT injured by fear catabolizes into *blame*.
36. OBEDIENCE overwhelmed by fear catabolizes into *fawningness*.
37. SURRENDER castrated by fear catabolizes into *submission*.
38. HAPPINESS hobbled by fear catabolizes into *discontent*.
39. JOYFULNESS disinherited by fear catabolizes into *dolefulness*.
40. SECURITY screwed by fear catabolizes into *instability*.
41. CHANGE challenged by fear catabolizes into *disquietude*.
42. SPEECH prefaced by fear catabolizes into *shrewdness*.
43. ORATORSHIP platformed by fear catabolizes into *artfulness*.
44. LEADERSHIP skippered by fear catabolizes into (a) *shipwreck*.

45. DISCRIMINATION hoodwinked by fear defects into (a) *hanging*.
46. DETACHMENT dispossessed by fear defects into *repudiation*.
47. FULLNESS scratched by fear defects into *unwholesomeness*.
48. EFFORT sustained by fear defects into *exhaustion*.
49. ACTIVITY damaged by fear defects into *half-heartedness*.
50. MEEKNESS mounted by fear defects into *timidity*.
51. HUMILITY hunched by fear defects into *humiliation*.
52. HONESTY hosted by fear defects into *hypocrisy*.
53. SINCERITY singed by fear defects into *simulation*.
54. SEX shanghaied by fear defects into *shame*.
55. PURITY prostituted by fear defects into *desire*.

56. FAME faulted by fear permutates into *fate*.
57. FORTUNE fallowed by fear permutates into *haplessness*.
58. FRIENDSHIP fouled by fear permutates into *wariness*.
59. RELATIONSHIP adulterated by fear permutates into *estrangement*.
60. FREEDOM fracassed by fear permutates into *despotism*.
61. ACCOMPLISHMENT acidized by fear permutates into *deprecation*.
62. INTELLIGENCE interloped by fear permutates into *involution*.
63. INNOCENCE inundated by fear permutates into *guilt*.
64. IMMORTALITY mutated by (subtle) fear permutates into *mortality*.
65. PARADISE infiltrated by fear permutates into *suffering*.
66. The HUMAN SOUL disfigured by fear permutates into *incarnation*.

67. SPIRIT keloided by fear sinks into *contraction*.
68. SILENCE disrupted by fear sinks into *sound*.
69. SOUND disturbed by fear sinks into *speech*.
70. LIGHT discolored by fear sinks into *shadow*.
71. KNOWLEDGE knurled by fear sinks into *ignorance*.
72. JUSTICE jousted by fear sinks into *injury*.
73. MONAD nudged by fear sinks into *I am*.
74. AHAMKARA poisoned by fear sinks into *pride*.
75. MAN mandated by fear sinks into *godlessness*.
76. GOD devirginized by fear sinks into *religion*.
77. (The) WORK impugned by fear sinks into (the) *black brotherhood*.

The Law of the Spirit demands that you lay down your defenses and stand denuded before God and Guru, until your personal psyche becomes *omnipotently* Open, *hopelessly* Helpless, and *heroically* Harmless.

The Brightness of BEING Lights-up the All-That-Is with the All of LOVE.

No discomfiture, no difficulty, no distress can triumph over; no vexation, no mortification, no persecution can prevail upon; no passion, no ache, no pain can conquer; no depression, no desolation, no crucifixion can crush; no dissatisfaction, no discontent, no anxiety can gain the upper hand; no terrible atrocity, no abject defeat can vanquish the rigorous Lover of the Infinite Light of the Great Immeasurable IMMENSITY.

We are all Godly Genies in a body-bottle.

However, we are so corked-up, worked-up and screwed-up that GOD-*as-the-Genie* within everyone just goes on sitting upon *His Blue Dais* within the Heart, naively blissed-out, sweetly-smiling, and outrageously un-Recognized.

Meanwhile, the personality proper, pounds out one private drama after another, to the high-profile pulse of self-importance.

If the *Godly-Genie* within is disparagingly disbelieved, unabashedly avoided, or repeatedly repudiated, then the magical *body-bottles* which naturally belong to both Bobby and Betsie, would eventually become bare, blithe bungalows that Life merely inhabits, or more grievously, they may just tergiversate and go AWOL, and breakup into bitter and broken abodes of blissful, bifurcated Blindness.

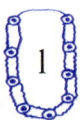

If you disinterestedly desire to die, the BUDDHA as your Benevolent Benefactor, *is obligated to bump you off.*

In the *blessed bloodbath* which follows, He must mercifully butcher all of your bodies into a state of Unborn.

If you collapse the cross of Time you instantly become an empty emitter of that Eternal Energy which renders you transcendentally timeless upon the passage of the CHRIST *crossing the long lavender stretch of the quintessential Emptiness of Absolute Space.*

Do not make much bones over the flesh; rather, make bones about the *Bodhicitta Breeze* breezing about your bones.

Have you really wondered why your eyes see what they see as the obvious and apparent truth, and not something else more radiantly Real and radically Empty, instead?

p

The emotional body is an unthinking babe; and the mental body is a thinking bore.

q

Emotions are essentially E-motion... *(i.e., energy in motion).*

The illumined sadhaka sees emotions as astral cloudbursts of mere personality expression, whilst he himself stands clear as a mindful point of consciousness in the Infinite Void, which stretches out subjectively spacious as his innate, very Empty Sky.

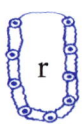

r

If somehow the All-of-It is *mystically* me, should I not simply begin upon the Dharma Path with the rudimentary rule of self-acceptance?

If somehow the Whole-of-It is *occultly* me, should I not realize that the All-of-It, that is, the Buddha, the Dharma, the Sangha, the world, and me... were already-always completely Innocent, yet somehow bonded by something strangely Sacrificial, right from the beginless start?

Memory is a modular-like multiple of mortally mummified images, mimeographing movement through the dummy animation of a mendaciously assumed mind munching on multiple, meaningless meanings through the moment-to-moment manifestation of an impermanent, menial 'me'.

Memory is about something of which the expiration date is past due, but of which a deluded one such as 'I' tries to re-inspire, or revive preciously today, without the wallop of the *weal,* (I mean, real), world.

Memory is something that died yesterday, and whose ghost distracts the moment, and pervades today.

Memory collects to itself the encrusting dust of past events, and perversely prevents the liberating perfume of the always-already New, from permuting the photonic present with the punch of the SOUL's Pure Impact.

In order to see afresh with each breath the disciple excises yesterday's worst, forgets the best, and lets go of all the rest.

The framework of friend and foe is forever forged by a fond filiation of foretoken fortune or fatal fall... of force and frailty, of fervor and fire, of fosterage and fang.

The framework of friend and foe is forever forged by a fond filiation of fine family or ferocious foemen... of faithfulness and faithlessness, of forbearance and foreboding, of freedom and feudality.

The framework of friend and foe is forever forged by a fond filiation of fostering fidelity or fulsome false-heartedness... of fair-play and foul-play, of fact and fib, of flawlessness and foible.

The framework of friend and foe is forever forged by a fond filiation of fervent feeling or fundamental frostiness... of foresight and fatalism, of friendship and fireworks, of forgiveness and farewell.

He who desolately scours LIFE for Love is likened to someone who desperately scratches for pure air while standing in the midst of the Great Outdoors smoking up a storm.

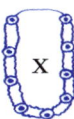

You must pay highly for mortal love, and to top it all, it keeps you *only-on-condition*.

You may lose all for Immortal Love, but it frees you, unequivocally, *under-all-conditions*.

Human love waxes and wanes in harrying humiliation to *condition* and *desire*.

Divine Love stands forever steadfast in the honing Humility of *submission* and *fire*.

The uncultivated heart falls headlong into hardness and dryness.

The Cultivated Heart falls headlong into Liquid Lava and Love.

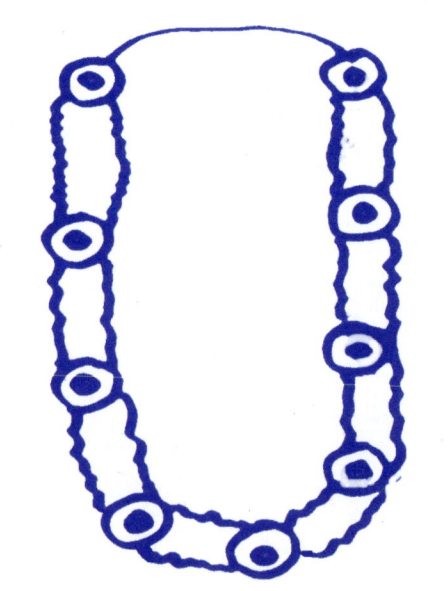

Beholdings

VIII

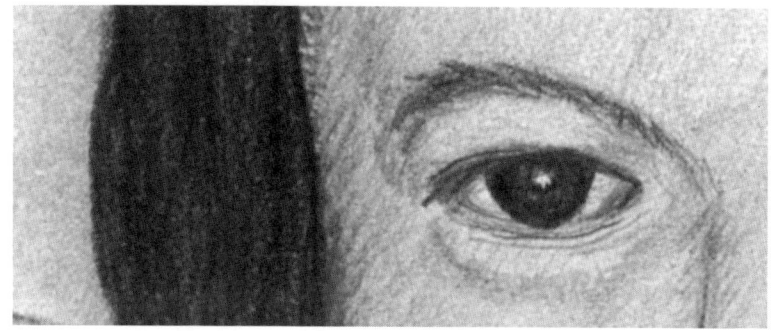

The Smiling Forehead
Paradoxes from Dadi to Daughter

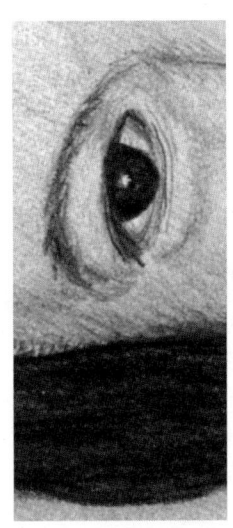

Beholdings

Be meek-minded for you are made of dirt, dust, and duty.

Be high-minded for you are made of Dignity, Divinity, and Dharma.

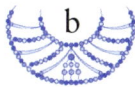

You cannot cross Heaven on a camel of sand.

You cannot shoot through the Celestine Blue with the Rocket Man in your pocket.

Happiness only happens when the *now* hails the *here* happily-happening, no mattering the *happenstance*.

Happiness happily holstered heartily hallows the humming, holy homophony of the Heart.

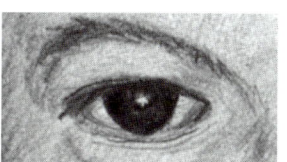

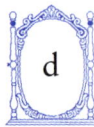

The heart healed by Hari's heed and Hare's heat is held up high by Heaven as the Holy Host of HRIDAYAM.

Impure intention importunes illegitimacy and invites ill-winds.

Immaculate intention invokes integrity and imposes imperturbability.

The sadhaka's spirit should be stripped of strife and filled with uncontested Life.

Same, similar *tell-tale* thoughts trek through the lower mind day-in, day-out, in a reeling mindset of endless, pointless repetition of self-delighting demands and thwarted narcissistic needs; and on and on they go, perpetually feeding ego-nurturing proclivities, and continually engaging in won or defeated desires; and they do so, with a sounding of their horns for the trophy of triumphant passion, or sadly, for the hampered hunger of self for necessitous, bawdy satisfaction.

Ah the omnipresent cries and hurried hurrahs by prurient libertines for an openly-expressed libidinousness, or for a free libertinism, when in reality none of it has anything to do with true Liberty, or authentic Liberation, or real Freedom.

This poor pilgrimage of *tell-tale* thoughts speaks significantly of the victimized ego's *"what if's"* and *"if only's"*.

These intemperate *tell-tale* thoughts spill out pell-mell into the wishy-washy wishes and wanton wants of the self.

These sorry *tell-tale* thoughts tearfully tear out of the sorrowful self, acrimonious cries of memories unforgotten, and of moments all too bitterly, still unforgiven.

These lamenting *tell-tale* thoughts also speak of remembered past times, and sometimes, of long ago lives... for which a person's mind achingly pines for (again), or else wistfully wishes that such and such a thing, or event, should not have happened... once upon a time.

Ah, of what rarity is the crystal clear mind denuded of any addictive memory and divested of all inner dispute.

Ah, of what exquisite beauty is the Spiritual TRUTH of a Pure and Unadulterated Emptiness.

It stands so unabashedly Naked.

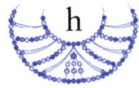

Buddha's SHUNYATA spawns a sparkling spontaneity of Beingness into the awakened space of the Non-Self.

Shiva's SILENCE soundlessly spanks the soul into serviceful submission with the primordial paddle of Spanda.

Temporal thinking thoughtlessly throbs to the thrills and thrash of a thousand thralls, though it still thirsts tenaciously.

Temporal thinking teems about in a tizzy for any trace of that titanic taskmaster, tentatively tautologized as the One Taste of Total TRUTH.

Instead of our mind being quite naturally a clear Buddha-Field of Divine endeavor, it resembles rather, a blatant, bloody war-zone of untempered cogitation and intemperate, mental thought.

Do sweep clean the mine-field of the mean and middling mind.

Eventful Experience, or Enriching Event, plus
Encircling E-motion and Enlivened Enjoyment, leads to
Energy Encapsulement, or Exalted Ennoblement, resulting in
Entity Enslavement, or Entity Enlightenment, et al.

O Brahman, blast my brain with a burst of Thy Bright.
Blitz my mind blind of all hinder and bind.

Blackout all blab and blat, bickering and brawl.
Bridle my bilge and bigotry, and bong bewitchingly Thy Bell.

Bellow Thy Name brilliantly and boldly into my body beautiful,
And burst Thy bedazzling Breath burning into my blood.

O Brahman, batter my body, break my back, and betroth my bones.

Behold my blustering bearing as bankrupt and bare;
And my brainsick blinkings as bland and Buddha-blank.

O Brahman, baptize me as Born-again.
Bodefully bless my Becoming and bury me in Basic Bliss.

O Brahman, I bid Thee, bedrape me as forever beguiled
By Thy Blazing Burnish and Thy Abiding Beauty.

Brazenly bestride me, and benignly, let Thy brassy Beam
Blush bountifully and broad upon my blazoned brow.

In the mean man there is mostly memory, a little Light.

In the advanced man there is no memory, only Light.

Some burning memories munch on mean beans, and munch, and munch, and munch till the belly becomes bitterly bloated and bodingly round; and until the beans are spilled and the stale gas is expelled, such memories but batter the blood with a relentless resentment; and bombast the brain with a bizarre behavior and a bent bravura; and generally make of Life a closed abode bearing a broken heart.

Such a harmed heart opens but momentarily, blushingly, (dispairingly), upon the glamorous smile of an opposite, more-like-it, more (seemingly) digestible, yum-yum memory of *maya* to yet munch on.

No memory, good nor bad, ever gets properly digested (in the average man); they, *(memories)*, just keep poppin' up like golden-buttered popcorn, or black-burnt toast, in the mind-brain; and the consciousness suffers the constant eructation of either a sweet, or bitter, (cyclic) remembrance.

The advanced man *remembers* not a memory; rather, he *re-calls* a memory, and then mindfully *releases* it every time.

Hold-on, and you are held up helplessly as you hole-up hopelessly, *(in hell)*.

Let go, and you are on the go aggressively as you go-go eagerly, *(to God)*.

The Fire of Awareness sets ablaze the serpent rope of all binding memory, and reduces the whole mnemonic bank to sacred White Ash.

The Teaching taunts you tirelessly to track Truth to the utter termination of the trail.

Then only, will God rise from where He Sat upon His Tat, and take you hOMe at last.

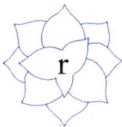

The Guru takes you to GOD; then GOD takes you unto Himself, and It's ADIEU.

GOD-Realization is a process of SELF-Revelation, not a book of self-Instruction.

The probationary pupil, once Purusha-impressed, can nevermore press his peaceable 'Preceptor-Protector' to precipitate a separation.

"Salutations to the unsaved!"

The Savior savors and swaddles those lost, more Sweetly still, in His Saviorness!

Get lost, not in sense, but in Self.
Get going, not in greed, but in God.

Get with it, not in wishes and wants, but in the world,
as a wailing White Whip.

The Satguru tells it as It Is:

"To tentatively touch the tinkling tittle of the Teacher's tiny toe, is to intrepidly trip the ting-a-ling trammels of an Eternal Trust."

But to thoroughly transfix with a tingling tenderness the total Foot, is to inevitably toe the living Mark of Truth.

Good dream, bad dream, life is but a Dream.

"Wake-up, child, and roar like the Lion of God you truly are, to devour the dream of Today!"

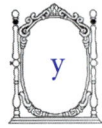

All personal *experiences* are but mind-crumbs hungrily caught up by the worldly mendicant who has never had a mouthful, (yet alone a meal), of Pure Manna at Mother Mary's Mansion of Divine Ministerings.

Shakti minus self is simply SHIVA Shivering on the summits.

Dangling Dilemmas

IX

The Smiling Forehead

Paradoxes from Dadi to Daughter

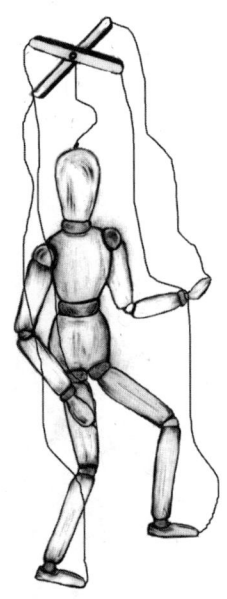

Dangling Dilemmas

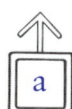

The karmic crunch of coiling, colliding clusters of cloudy concern, customary conflict and configured chaos, crashes innocuously and incuriously into the cosmic Calm of a sadhaka's *cultivated* Consciousness.

The penumbra of pain cannot comfortably contort itself under an umbrella of Light.

The darkness of disease cannot snuggle, bundle-up and abide in a body full of Bright.

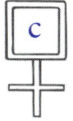

A compassionate *outer* smile shyly suggests the serene poise of the Inner Self.

A tranquil, *inner* smile dispassionately bestirs the impassioned nature of the SELF's, Radiant Emptiness.

Dangling Dilemmas

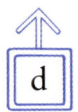

Dare to diligently dispel the dilemma of dualism by developing a diffident but definite doggedness of unitive duality.

Dare to deftly defy the dilemma of dichotomy by developing a driving but devout dispassion vis-à-vis discernible division.

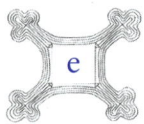

Personally prehended pain and pleasure provide a podium for the pupil and pilgrim upon the Path to play an important part in the personal *purification* and impersonal *spiritualization* of the planet.

Primo, in perfect point and *quid pro quo* counterpoint, to the prodigious Plan of our planet's present, Peerless PRECEPTOR.

Secundo, in perfect propriety to the Pure Purpose of the whole Galaxial Production, compassionately put on by the PARA PARAM PURUSHA... *the* ONE *about* Whom Naught Can Be Said.

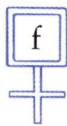

In the very moment you pithily *apprehend* your Empty Nature, you immediately understand that you are conditionally-Free.

In the mini-second you unequivocally *know* (that) your existence is Absolutely Not, you instantly realize your Un-conditional Freedom.

In the *Eternal Twinkle* (that) you slip into the Sambhogakaya State, you are irrevocably, Sat-Chit-Ananda, Free.

In the *Awakened Absence* of time you realize that you Are Irretrievably Naught, and have always been THAT, you are suddenly Always-Already Free.

You then magically find yourself sitting on the living lap of Samantabhadra, in that very same, beginningless, ongoing creative moment when the Dharmakaya sparked the Dharmata, and mercurially transmogrified Non-Being into BEING.

The probable provenance of a problem is in the *present-past*.
The principle plumbing of a problem is in the *present-present*.
The proper preventing of a problem is in the *present-predicative*.

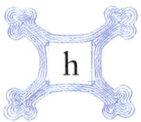

The DISCIPLE must slack down, shake off, and suspend *sadness*.
The INITIATE must deplume, drum out, and dump *despair*.

OF SUCH IS THE DISCIPLINE ON THE PATH:

A disciple must not be slowed down by, nor unduly parade, an apparent tamasic state.

All terrible temptations and dark trips, must never ever vociferate a repetitive, triumphant note.

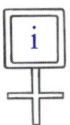

Individual unhappiness is the cinereous cirrhosis of an existence soiled, sphacelated and despoiled by the small self's scurrile swindling of the subleasing of Life to the pretextual principle of desire.

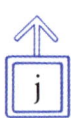

A predisposed predilection to that which is pleasing tends to propel the prejudice of a person to that which is primarily pleasant, and fails to polarize him to Mankind's planetary orb of *One Pulse of Plural Pain*.

All too often the word *attachment* harbors a hidden addiction.

All too often the word *precious* packs an underhanded drunk punch.

All too often the word *passion* purports a presumed payola.

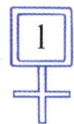

As per the breaching of any pre-incarnational occult contract of *relational import,* it may be of interest for the sadhaka to note that upon the Upward and Evolutionary Path, the following negative effects and affects may take place, vis-à-vis a seriously broken (esoteric) agreement of sexual signification:

The price of an illegitimate passion is the likely cost of causing others inordinate pain.

The sin of an ongoing and unlawful sexual transgression is the potential abasement of self and other.

The punishment for selfish and wrongful pleasure is the ignorant torture of Truth and the probable birth of misery.

The result of illicit sense-satisfaction, or of any abject self-indulgence, is the instant diminishment of the Light within the head and heart, and a provisional stoppage of Spiritual progress.

As to an Initiate's implicit part in any improper play, it may be correct to say that he un-sagely seduced his innocent senses into seeking divine offence of his Sacred Samayas.

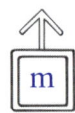

The *discerning* disciple perceives that even a paradisal pleasure encapsulates the purveyance of a craving, albeit, presumably celestial.

The *detached* disciple apprehends the true Abode of Being as being absolutely beyond any ecstatic Behavioral Bliss; and absolutely above all the pleasurable ploys of happenstancial Happiness.

The *Delivered* Disciple has explicitly determined that the only proper, primal, and pristine proclamation of Being is an emancipated, empty Paean of JOY.

The sugary epithet of '*my dear*' often harbors within the mind, a detached, distancing fear.

The honeyed style of '*my sweets*' often encloses within the heart, a soft but secreted sorrow.

The common designation of '*my darling*' often covertly encodes within the being, the deepest, adumbrated disenchantment, (time and time again).

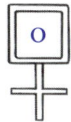

Sadness is the somber, ashy, often unforeseen shadow of disappointed desire, coupled to a disillusioned facet of destiny.

Sadness circumscribes a subject around which the personality self has a surreptitiously selfish expectancy; or at least, a slight sliver of a hopeful prospect of either personal happiness, or some semblance of self-serving satisfaction.

Sadness is mainly a malady of what can be called 'the bliss of the blues', catering unwholesomely to the emotional body; and turning the personality self immaturely and selfishly inward, in an involuntary downspin of atmospheric doubt, surly discouragement, and secret despair.

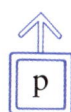

There is no drunken deluge like an impassioned desire; no obfuscated cataract like a constant craving.

There is no dire delirium like a bovine devotion; no purblind predilection like a preferred passion.

There is no greater deception than a magnetic delusion; no more mindless ignorance than a credible illusion.

There is no dirtier disclosure the likes of a double-dealing disloyalty; no more torturous hell than the flinted righteousness of a hallowed hatred.

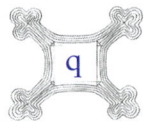

The True Teacher's trail is at once thought-less and trackless.

The Sai Samurai's sword slices once indivisibly, and twice ecstatically.

The Saintly Sadhu's sojourn is nowhere to be found in his spiritual itinerary.

The Wise and Wizened Wali's wayfaring is wholly of wind, wing, and whisper.

The Bu-tai Buddha's big-bellied body is made of lots and lots of enlightened Bodhicitta and empty Bare Breath.

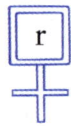

He who ignorantly greets the glowingly garrulous as being necessarily nimble-witted and wily-wise, is indeed, a gravely gullible gudgeon.

He who moronically mistakes mere loquacity for sagacity, is indeed, largely loco.

He who is glib and glitzy and has the gift of the gab, is given to gusto, guffaw, and great gas.

Solely that sadhaka who bodily-bears the cryptology of the TRUE TEACHING can become a true TEACHER... never the intelligent, (but oft delusional) specimen of a sadhaka, who simply talks (a lot) about the Teaching, (and about the Teacher), but stays ever, the effusive, albeit (*knowledgeable*), spiritual seeker.

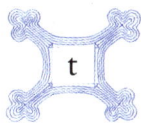

The secretive *Safari of the Seven Sages* spiritually signifies the selective stimulation and sacrificial safekeeping of all that is esoterically Sacred in the Universe.

The strange *Star-Stalking of the Seven Sages,* and Their silent sailings across the shunyata of space and down through the steeps of time, stay sempiternally unseen and ever undisclosed, even to the subtle sight of the good angels and proud gods.

Although the *Seven Seraphic Sages* subsist sempiternally unseen, They cosmically, occasionally, steal forth into our Universe with the sericeous footfalls of absolute Stealth, but only for some supremely sovereign, Absolutely Nameless, planetary benefit.

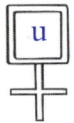

*A*ncient is oft arrogant, artificial, affected, and often assuming.
*H*oary is oft huffy, hypocritical, highfalutin, and often histrionic.
*O*ld is oft obtrusive, overnice, ornery, and often ostentatious.

*O*ld is not obligingly *overwise*. *O*ld is neither obligatorily *owlwise*.

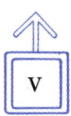

The Primal Precept of the PATH is *Pure PREMA*, or *Bodhicitta COMPASSION*.

The Proven Prescription of the PATH is *Disciplined PRACTICE*, or *Astute SADHANA*.

The Primary Procedure of the PATH is *Selfless PERFORMANCE*, or *Bodhisattva SERVICE*.

The Primordial Principium of the PATH is the *PARA PARAM PURUSHA*, or the *ADI BUDDHA*, as *LORD SAMANTABHADRA*.

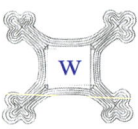

The Teacher tells the Tale; the Trainee tests its Truth.

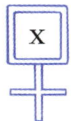

Although the INQUIRY is *individual*, the QUEST is *collective*.

Although the *seeker* solitarily comes to the TEACHER, the climb is without exception, *Communal*.

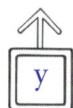

Train to pack upon your back the whole Mountain of PREMA, not just a few piddlin' pebbles of Love.

The devotee as Hanuman hoists high his backpack of pain and energetically hikes to the sweet Summit of Lord RAMA's Heart.

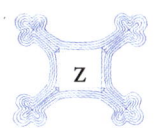

If, in the heedless pursuit of some selfish sensual pleasure, you inflict a deep injury upon another's real love, you unequivocally incur a karmic condition of solemn, crunching comparability.

Then, often and posthaste, a very sorry piece of Heaven plummets disquietingly down the serpentine, *prashchit* pipelines of (your) incarnated Consciousness.

Promptly thereafter, all temporal and unremorseful past paradisal pleasures, press-in and press-down ignobly, into the pits of a personally ominous night of dark, often inscrutable Divine Distress... perhaps lasting an entire lifetime, and ofttimes, being unequivocally uncomfortable, for much longer remedial periods.

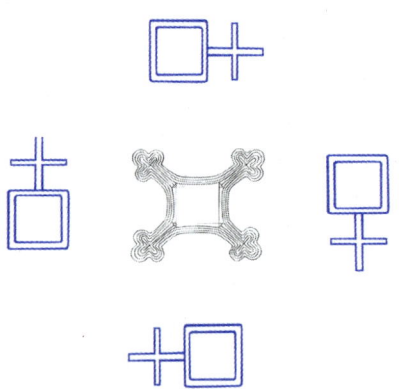

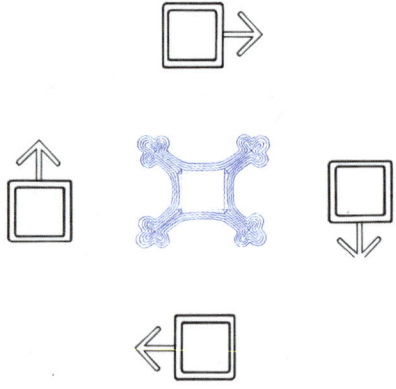

Stop! Halt! Whoa!

X

The Smiling Forehead

Paradoxes from Dadi to Daughter

Stop! Halt! Whoa!

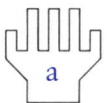

*S*top! *Halt! Whoa!* Hold everything and *be assuredly advised*:

"Both vice and virtue must be firmly vanquished."

*S*top! *Halt! Whoa!* Hold everything and *be keenly aware*:

"Individual potency is all-pervasive only because the Para Param Purusha is utterly Immanent."

*S*top! *Halt! Whoa!* Hold everything and *be stoutly briefed*:

"The Lord of Compassion can only Become One with you for the sake of other."

Stop! Halt! Whoa!

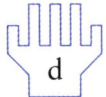

*S*top! Halt! Whoa! Hold everything and *be rightly counseled*:

"Once the disciple has trained himself to depend on Naught, he must perforce do his sadhana with even more unremitting emptiness."

*S*top! Halt! Whoa! Hold everything and *be sensitively guided*:

"In PHASE 1 of Spiritual Sadhana there are three principally negative *traits* to be detected, detoxed and deposed, from within the personality.

These are: *distress, deception,* and *dissoluteness.*

The *aspirant* must be trained to call ardently upon **D.D.D.**, that is, Detachment, Dharma, and Decency for all of the above's *spiritual cure* and gradual TRANSMUTATION."

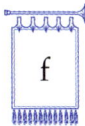

*S*top! *Halt! Whoa!* Hold everything and *be wisely mentored*:

"In PHASE 2 of Spiritual Sadhana there are equally three dominantly negative *characteristics* to be cognized and corrected within the **psyche**.

These are: *discouragement, depression,* and *disloyalty.*

The *probationary disciple* is again encouraged to patiently call upon **D.D.D.**, that is, Discrimination, Dispassion and Devotion for all of the above's *sacred cure* and eventual TRANSFORMATION."

*S*top! *Halt! Whoa!* Hold everything and *be swiftly liberated*:

"In PHASE 3 of Spiritual Sadhana there are also three predominantly negative *dimensions of mind* coveting a parasitic relationship with the **Soul**.

These are: *darkness, desolation,* and *despair.*

The *accepted disciple* must more than ever diligently and occultly call on **D.D.D.**, that is, (on) Divinity, Dominion and Delight for all of the above's definite and final TRANSFIGURATION."

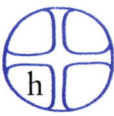

*S*top! *Halt! Whoa!* Hold everything and *be preeminently prompted*:

"The one task of the disciple is to consciously make of Divinity the living reality of *this* world."

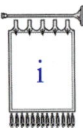

*S*top! *Halt! Whoa!* Hold everything and *clearly understand*:

"No matter how grand, glorious and glorified is Spiritual Sadhana, the personal psyche's peregrine syndrome of relentlessly trekking the *ups and downs* of the one hundred mountains, one thousand hills, and ten thousand hillocks, remains still, the rough *natural terrain* of the PATH."

"The lovely *valleys* are but the validated dowries of graded spiritual effort."

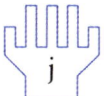

*S*top! *Halt! Whoa!* Hold everything and *be valorously inspired*:

"Aspire potently and you shall eventually reel-in a spiritual experience of pure *Presence*."

"Aspire with punch, perseverance, presence and enterprise and you shall eventually pull in enough horsepower to empower a *Pure Heart*."

*S*top! *Halt! Whoa!* Hold everything and *reflect*:

"The planet Earth may possibly be Sanat Kumara's present orphan, but this poor planetary orphan is destined to become the ETERNAL KING's Summer Palace."

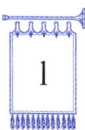

*S*top! *Halt! Whoa!* Hold everything and *know irrevocably that*:

"Real Love does not hang its hat on the coat-rack of common happiness."

"It hangs its Kingly Crown high upon the crossbars of *Sacrifice*."

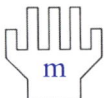

*S*top! Halt! Whoa! Hold everything and *be humbly absent*:

"True Love gives the gift of self away, for truly, there is no one home to be happy, or unhappy."

*S*top! Halt! Whoa! Hold everything, *be patient and realize*, (without a doubt), that:

"All things pass away, especially the pain of pleasure."

*S*top! Halt! Whoa! Hold everything and *be amply prepared*, (to cognize that):

"Only when the sadhaka has bravely borne the brunt of affront, aspersion, indignity and injury, can he occultly incur the sacred contract of comforting others Commandingly."

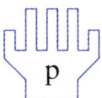

*S*top! *Halt! Whoa!* Hold everything and *intuitively grasp*:

"There is only one Religion, *God-in-Man*."
"There is only one Revelation, *God-as-Man*."

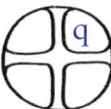

*S*top! *Halt! Whoa!* Hold everything and to be sure, *doubt not, nor waver not*:

"A misstep is symbolically always a significant step in the Sojourn."

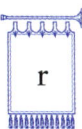

*S*top! *Halt! Whoa!* Hold everything and learn to *inviolably trust*:

"Trust that the Entire Truth is entrenched entirely as Essential Emptiness in the crown's Crown."

"Trust that Bodhicitta awakens naturally as a Radiant Emptiness in the Naught of Self."

"Trust that Om Mani Padme Hum is the sacred six syllable mantra of lucid Lokesvara's all emcompassing Heart of Compassion."

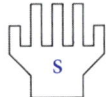

*S*top! *Halt! Whoa!* Hold everything and *become Divinely inflamed*, (knowing that):

"The *transformed* sadhaka can no longer be his own self; he has to become the Lord's Only Self, and his sole role is that of (the) Sanctified Slave."

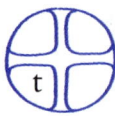

*S*top! *Halt! Whoa!* Hold everything and *be selflessly prepared*:

"The *experienced* sadhaka must compassionately empathize with those whose sights are still fixated upon the attractive force of the polarization of phenomenal opposites, such as pain and pleasure, happiness and sorrow, dark and light, and ultimately, life and death."

"The *tried* sadhaka, must furthermore, selflessly render to ordinary folks that inspirational hand which is so needed, in order to cope with the *ordinary, extraordinarily.*"

"The *advanced* sadhaka, for his part, must deal with the *all and everything*, impeccably, skillfully exercising Chenrezi's Heart-tool of compassionate, *detached attachment*, **Masterfully.**"

*S*top! Halt! Whoa! Hold everything and *unconditionally admit*:

"Once an accepted Disciple you matter little."

"Truth matters markedly much; but what really matters, is Nothing at all."

*S*top! Halt! Whoa! Hold everything and *sweetly smile*:

"There can be no new Stuff, only a fresh *leela* of the Lord to digest and dance to; and a whole new *original face* to laugh with, in spontaneously generated Joy."

*S*top! Halt! Whoa! Hold everything and *be strongly astute*:

"On the Path of POWER there is no such thing as spiritual phenomena and *a warrior's wand*; there is only GOD acting with ENERGY and FORCE through the empty corpse of *a dynamic disciple*."

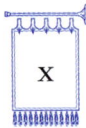

*S*top! *Halt! Whoa!* Hold everything and *ponder spaciously*:

"Many are (the) tentative truths, but One Only Is... *the Truth*."

"All truth theorems and spiritual serums must be bounded up into one big bundle as *B.S.*, before any REALIZATION of Reality can radically burst through the postmodern, mystical bubble of our *ego-ratified* Babylonian Beatitude."

*S*top! *Halt! Whoa!* Hold everything and be *shamelessly counted and Rejoice*:

"The Soul salivates with Love over a spoonful of spinach soup."

"All substance and situation, even the most usual and simple, is spiffy stuff for the Soul's spontaneity to resolve into an enticing, etheric equation, or spiritual resolution."

"If the sadhaka would only learn to spiritually trust and make creative use of the Soul's Spontaneity in all situational solving, he would in due time, do away with all temporal stress, strain, and solicitude."

"Consequently, in his not ever wasting Vital Force, but rather, intelligently gathering *essential Energy* into himself, he could, eventually, consciously develop the crucial capacity and required strength, to be of real *Sacrificial Service* to sentient mankind."

*S*top! *Halt! Whoa!* Hold everything and *become the galvanized gladiator*:

"If S\ptext, would set about to straighten out all situations, the world would surely be a *no Show*.

There would be no spontaneity, no progress, and no longer would Spirit be interested to excess emptiness into matter.

There would be only powdered pistachio, plastic pizza and phenomenally-pained and painted puppetry.

There would be only a spiritual cyclorama of clones, divinely-undone and awfully alone.

May the Buddha save mankind from spiritual interference, and so-called, compassionately Divine intervention!"

In conclusion, do all with Buddha doing through you, until He Does all with you doing nothing, and (yet) Accomplishing everything, purely on Empty.

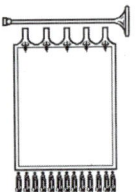
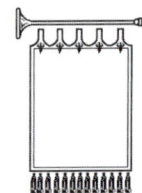
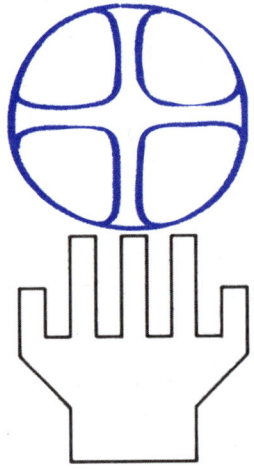
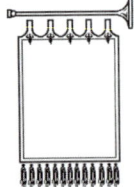
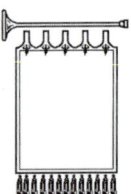

Sword and Sanctity

XI

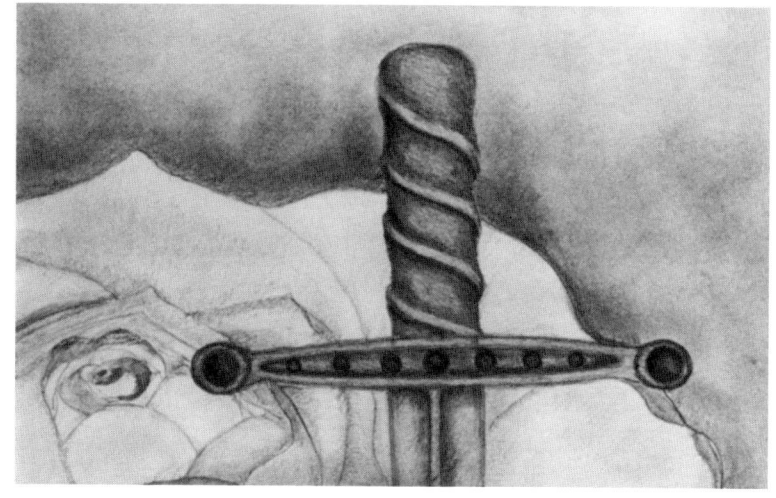

The Smiling Forehead
Paradoxes from Dadi to Daughter

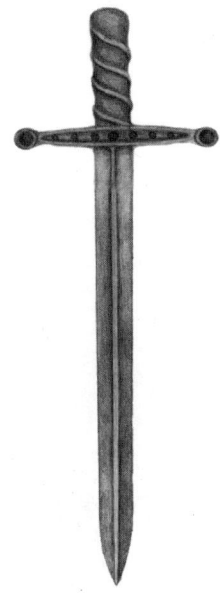

Sword and Sanctity

Lightly skim the rim of Saraswati's *quickening* skirt.
Scoot-up the steep crags to ascetic Shiva's solitary summit.
Spread the wings of Self to the infinitude of the Lost Horizon.
Bravely scale Lord Indra's impassioned scattering sky, formlessly fashioned from a fiery-bolted emptiness of Lightning Clarity.
Shoot-out your Spirit through Sri Krishna's fathomless Spatial Blue.
Boldly snatch an orphaned star from Jolly Jupiter's nirvanic nimbus.

Go ahead, slack-jaw the CREATOR's spatio-temporal spectrum.
And like Hari Hari, steal spiritedly Home to your own Heart.

Of course, all of the foregoing can only happen while you are solidly swamped at Work, with a super-yummy Subramanya submarine sandwich close at hand, for the five-minute lunch break.

The principle opposition to pragmatic spirituality on the phenomenal plane, is not the pulling down of the esoteric spiritual sciences into a semblance of clarity in consciousness.

It is rather, the skillful putting down into an exoteric mode of sadhana the almost perfect Inner Plan, upon a mostly imperfect paper of phantom physicality.

Sword and Sanctity

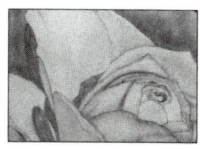

Man pugnaciously protects his imperfections and purposefully puts off the purification portion of the *spiritualization process*, for fear of a permanent permutation being impressed upon his familiar personal psyche.

To presuppose the purificatory process with an open and unprejudicial Mind, as being a peremptory pivoting point of the Pathway which plunges the pupil headlong to purview the Primordial Perspective, purely pivots the pupil's protracted personality towards the polestar of a more permanent Prajna, and the inspiriting promise of a pertinent, primary Peace.

To live the life of an ordinary man is for those who are *radically-Free*, a physical twister, an emotional tornado, a mental hurricane, and notwithstanding, a S<small>OUL</small> breeze.

The All of Life is played out on some long-forgotten island of Bliss, whirling upon a planetary piece of terrestrial peace, somewhere lost, in some nowhere-to-be found intradimensional Christmas corridor of Empty Space.

To live the life of a commonly-contracted man is for the *radically-Released*, a temporal tempest, a physical typhoon, an emotional earthquake, a mental agony, a burning Causal-bush, and of course, a pleasurable Monadic journey into the pulsing spaciosity of time.

When the solemn TRUTH finally does crack Its sweet smile upon the Soul, it is usually because Divine WISDOM has Lighted-up the empty *mind,* with dazzling diamond-droplets of HEART-Bliss.

It is more meritful for the pupil to persevere on his particular Spiritual Path, in spite of happenstance and problem, of mishap and doubt, of calamity and contestability, than it is to scrap his present progress, and have to polarize his puny personality to Lord Maitreya's contraposed disputation of WHY?

The Divine afterglow of the Divine afterclap composes the afterimage of SAMANTABHADRA, which leaves an aftereffect of Bliss and an aftertaste of TRUTH, after whose aftermath of Pure Empty Intensity, the spiritual experience of the pupil is proscripted with a prodigal aftergrowth of pure COMPASSION for all sentiency.

Desire a thing, and it hurts.
Get the thing, and it (still) hurts.
Lose the thing, and it hurts, even more.

To make naught of no-thing while aspiring to nothingness, and to untie the knot of everything as it spontaneously arises, comes near to the Nuclear Naught of all things.

Everything of naught that perhaps ought to have been, but never got to be, never took natural root in appearance, because neither this, nor that, ever existed before *things* just spontaneously arose.

The essence of Naught imperceptibly sighs into the Great Immensity, as none other than the ecstatic and radiant Emptiness of the Infinitely Indigo, Imponderable VOID.

The masked muckraker who mindlessly and maliciously mudslings muck and mire at a harmless man's meek mug, will himself be mugged by matching mechanical karma, and marked in methodical, mathematical measure by meticulous samsara.

All things have a natural bent and bias, *Impermanence*.
All things have a pronounced ply and predisposition, *Disappointment*.

All things aim for an improbable prejudice and propensity, *Happiness*.
All things delight in a spontaneous proclivity, *Joyfulness*.

All things tend towards an ecstatic and startled star, the *Original Face*.

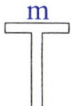

The Machiavellian man who deliberately disseminates mythomaniac mendacities and who issues defamatory misstatements, and who slings sanctimonious misinterpretations, and who meanly marrs and harmfully miscolors the sacred character of a good man, obviously manifests a misfeasant, mismanaged mind, which is mockingly marked as *marijuana gold* by the smoldering, flesh-smoking Lord Yama.

Because of a bent bias for better and best objects and objectives, an unbroken bounty of bloody blows obdurately bonks the being, embitters the beak, and finally, breaks the back.

Emboldened by the unspoken bill of an individual's birthing right for a body beautiful, and blindly backed by the mayic rule of the ego's existential demand for the forever-binding, all of the aforementioned best *objects and objectives* seem to abide bullheadedly as bare and abject wish-fulfillment, and they tend to benefit only their obvious bossman and blessed beneficiary — the insubstantial 'I'.

The business of the basic belief in *me* and the narcissistic braggadacio of 'my' and 'mine', bodes for some bad times and sad stuff, for the typical pupil upon the path.

All of this, of course, can only happen in relative time, some long, haughty stretch before the recurrent *bel canto* requiem of the *Buddha's Burning Breath*, conclusively convinces the sadhaka to come, (at last), crestfallen and bitterly broken, to his own Bodhi tree of Enlightened Vision and Empty Reapings.

Truth is about the only thing that you cannot easily desire, acquire, or lose.

Truth is an invisible, potent fire of unqualified Isness, and Its flames are but naked tongues of Empty Spirit.

Sword and Sanctity

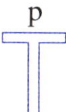

The *sanctity* of the Saint and the *sword* of the Samurai are conjoined archetypal expressions of an imminently perfect *Peace* and perfect *Justice* upon earth... one being inescapable and the other indispensable... for the evolutionary movement of Man to reach a completion.

The successful sadhaka must become both saint and samurai in one steadfast, disciplined strategy of Life Accomplishment, coupled to a natural Consummate Emptiness.

The *frieze* of *fixity* must be fractured, felled and fatally flattened, if the effervescent force of Spontaneous Freshness is to be naturally conjured, and proceed onwards in being radically active and positively transformative, in the creatively dynamic, decrystalization process of Consciousness.

'If you rightly alter your attitude you positively alter your altitude.'

Only after the needed aforementioned alteration has been accomplished, can you then rightly administer your spontaneous All-Attention everywhere, and therefroth, positively administer your rule of pansophic, wise authority over your lifeplan and its polymorphous relationships in relative time.

The Lord will not reveal Himself to you until you have unequivocally *proffered* and *surrendered* yourself to the ineluctable Onslaught of Life.

The Lord will not reveal Himself to you until you have learned the patience of waiting in a vulnerable suspension of breath... *for an entire Eternity of Hope.*

The Lord will not reveal Himself to you until you have learned to patiently stand in a perfect position of openness... *for the uncertain Inevitability of Faith.*

Uplifting but immature emotion prior to a real act of Creation, either chokes up in quiet desperation, or expires quickly like a love flame in a frenzied ecstasy.

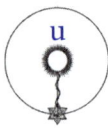

The Soul is not natural to earth; nor is matter at ease with Spirit.

Spirituality is not easy for the body to harpoon harmoniously, nor natural for the mind to lovingly assume.

INITIATION is not natural, nor is it innocent; it is not compassionate, nor is it nice; it is not angelic, nor is it human.

INITIATION is utterly unnatural, utterly unkind, and utterly unaccommodating; it is undeniably unsympathetic; it is undesirably unaffectionate and undeservedly inhuman; yet, it is Unadulteratedly Divine.

To stabilize spirit within the coat of matter is the quest of the Soul.

To stabilize the soul within the human habit is the assignment of Spirit.

To seal spirit and soul committed conjointly to corporeal matter and temporal mind is the occult contract of the Spontaneous, Free SELF.

The subjective, Inner Life must be intentionally and inventively liberated, before it can be invoked masterfully for the material sanctification of Evolution.

The involutionary forces relentlessly woo our weak wills to employ selfish thought and deploy impure motivation for material advancement, so much so, that a constant negative concentration of convolutionary tension is perforce, carried forth into our present moment of continually creative, but sometimes, aversely-polarized attention.

It may be significant to note that an ego-centered circumlocution of the consciousness, creates a labyrinthine, revolving revolution of self-obsession which somehow, surreptitiously ensures a continuation of the atomic body's incipient involution, within the sacrificial configuration of the Soul's concyclical evolution.

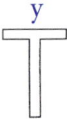

The enlightened future of a compassionate humanity rests upon the illuminary strength of mankind's liberal mixing of the basic substance of mammon with the universal solvent of Love's Light.

Upon the battlefield of a sadhaka's Soul sometimes ensues the vicious skirmish of a dynamic physical desire locked in contention with the exigency of a spiritually inspired activity.

The sadhaka's primary duty is to stay unalterably Calm, and well-esconsed within the Sacred Heart of his LORD.

As to whether he succeeds against a physically contentive desire, or succumbs to critical circumstance this once, is not really an issue of supreme significance.

What is of import, is that he continue to actively heed the Spirit's Call, and Recall, and continue to purely Love and demonstrate utter Compassion for his fellow man, with the sling-shot strength and the entire hope of a David's resolute faith in his LORD.

It is an accepted *sine qua non* that for the experienced and tried sadhaka, there is no such thing as spiritual failure, and this remains resolutely so, even if he dies discouragingly and completely destitute upon the fiery cross of Circumstance… once upon a lifetime.

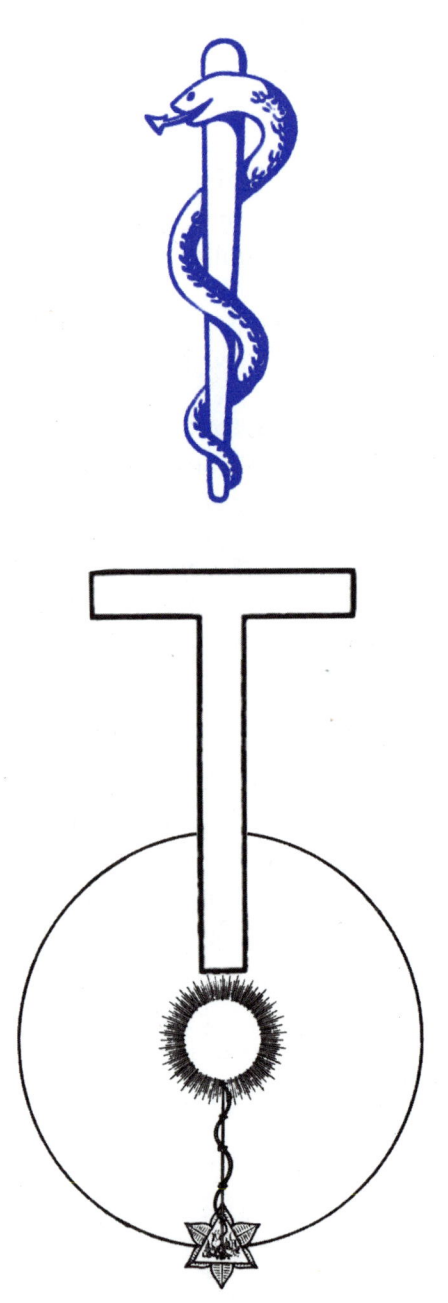

Stalwart Sadhakas & Disciplined Disciples

XII

The Smiling Forehead
Paradoxes from Dadi to Daughter

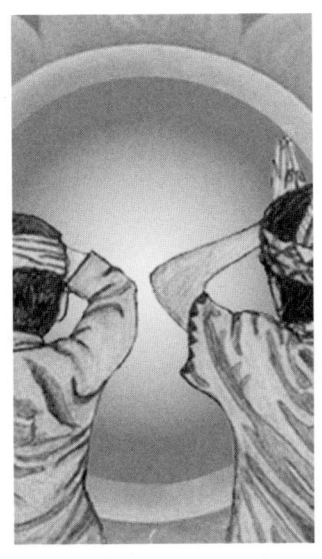

Stalwart Sadhakas & Disciplined Disciples

The stalwart sadhaka must stretch himself out coldly upon the Lord's rack of Light.

He must ruthlessly dig-up and display all defects, deficiencies and damages done to his self and to his otherselves.

He must seek out, lay bare, and confess all of his faults, weaknesses, imperfections, blemishes, vices, shortcomings, and sins.

He must envision clearly all of the aforementioned in his consciousness and he must correctly censure them; he must rightly rebuke, reproach and reject their delinquency, their spiritual impropriety, without the least self-indulgence and without guilt.

He must be self-cognizant, self-contrite, self-chastised, and allow for glad change.

In perfect Joy the stalwart sadhaka must accurately agonize, do tollgate tapasya, and serve time.

The disciplined disciple must cheerfully claim the crucifixion. He must gladly give hosanna to the Father's cruel Clap upon the crown; he must simultaneously suffer and celebrate, the excruciating Clasp of the Christ upon his contrite consciousness.

The disciplined disciple will be harrowed and he will hurt; yet he must huzzah and shout Hosanna!

The disciplined disciple will learn to burn and be reduced in consciousness to Sacred Ash; yet throughout the whole ordeal he must Brightly bear it all; and he must sweetly smile all the while, during the test, trial and third degree process of the inner transformative, White Heat.

The disciplined disciple in surrendering to his Soul, will suffer the significant subtraction of substance from his existential *Aham*.

He will, subsequently, sublate his self to a total abstraction of the emptying of the ego upon the aceldamic anvil of acute experience, contraposed to compressed time and extended space.

The personalized platform of the Soul's progressive battle for spiritual supremacy takes place, of course, in direct concomitance to the disciplined disciple's greatly accelerated Karma, and yet, he must during the whole fiery while, learn to Godly-gleam, and be like a Lighted stream of Divinity, to all and to none.

The stalwart sadhaka must ermitely yearn for *yog* and leanly lean upon *sadhana*; and yet, he must contemplate, and boff like Obelix; meditate, and guffaw like Goofie; concentrate, and tee-hee-tittle like Olive Oyle.

The stalwart sadhaka must be able to boldly blitz into the most boundless Bliss, over and over again; and still, he must be able to silly sweet-smile like shy 'ole Minnie, meekly meeting the great Mahatma Mickey for the very first time, at Disney's super-magnificent 'Divinity Museum' of Looney Saints.

The disciplined disciple must discover that during the discontentment phase of the adolescent stage of his Spiritual development, the Master will not directly meddle in the miasmic dilemmas of his student's desire-dramas; but neither will the Teacher discount his disciple's hedonistic tendencies, nor disallow, any dubious or dastardly deed, to go unheeded, (and unrecorded).

In the Spiritual Adolescent stage of a disciple's unfoldment, the Master will, on the whole, consider it as (usually) improper to point out this or that defect, in the seditious sadhaka's sadhana, even if the faultfinding is done adroitly, or diplomatically.

The Master understands that if the sadhaka is unjudiciously driven during this disgruntled decanter of development, he may dumbly defect, and his discipleship be (possibly) compromised.

It is at this difficult crossroad, or degree of Divine development, that the disciple very (often) nearly drowns in the muddled waters of his own darkened karma.

It is often in such a mood of somewhat blind desperation, whilst stuck in a stark state of seemingly (complete) inner isolation, that the disciple appears, paradoxically, to be sympathetically forced by his own Soul to climb upon his Cross of Crisis, consciously.

It is only in the diligent Light of a disciple's (desolate) WILL, that the disobedient (spiritual) adolescent is driven to cry out to the destructive CHRIST for the radical SELF-transformation so desperately needed, upon his (personal) PATH of chosen Return.

The stalwart sadhaka seeks not a slight alteration of his spirit; he will settle for nothing less than the complete consubstantiation of his consciousness into the *radically* Impersonal and the *totally* Empty.

The disciplined disciple does not demand a mere modulation of the cogitation process but presses for the total mutation of his concrete mentation into that of a random Empty Mind.

The disciplined disciple stalks not the consciousness for the mere modification of the mind, but rather, for the metamorphoses of the mean mentality into the enlightened metanoia of an already absent and always timeless, spontaneous arising of the innate nature of Pure Mind.

The stalwart sadhaka dispassionately dives into the *ordinarily palpable* and *candidly ordinary,* as if it was the *impassionately extraordinary,* because he personally experiences the Pure Passion of PURUSHA for the ubiquitously common Heartbeat.

The disciplined disciple rightly recognizes that sexuality is circulating Shakti, money is shared Magnanimity, power is radiating Prema, and spirituality is (naught but) Self-Essence; and that finally, enlightenment is nothing but the radiant showering of a clearly, Emanated Emptiness.

The stalwart sadhaka sagely sees that SEX is essentially selfish, and sex is swayable; and yet, on the other hand, sex screens a sacred intent and encodes a significant secret.

The stalwart sadhaka sagely sees that MONEY is magnetic, and money is malleable; and yet, on the other hand, money moves a momentous momentum of matter, materially mattering very much.

The stalwart sadhaka sagely sees that POWER is persuasive, and power is plastic; and yet, on the other hand, power permits a high-priority protean politics, as well as a purposeful progression of the populace toward the fulfillment of the Plan.

The stalwart sadhaka sagely sees that true SPIRITUALITY is selfless, steadfast and sempiternal in its service proferred to the Solitary Supreme. Yet, on the other hand, true SPIRITUALITY acts practically on the physical plane by occultly severing the shackles of both secular slavery and restrictive sectarianism.

The disciplined disciple rightly savvies that the Spirit of the *Second Self* will always seek to stretch the consciousness of the Soul to Its extreme extensibility of Incarnated Veracity.

The awakened *Second Self,* under the auspices of the ONE WITHOUT A SECOND, will through Its own Herculean VOLITION, mercilessly steer the infinitely servable Soul into a substantial, shepherded serfdom of perpetually *surveyed Spirituality*.

This ongoing surveyance of the *spiritualization* process will impose itself without pity upon the Soul and Its *sukshamas,* (vehicles of expression), until the True Purpose of *jivatmic* incarnation has been achieved through the initiatory merit of *Revelation.*

Only thereafter, can Absolute Power be thus considered safe to descend through the Soul's Fontanelle, and made to dance upon the *Enlightened Brow* of Its host body, the *awakened, individualized, empty* Consciousness.

The stalwart sadhaka recognizes that whilst SPIRIT directly intends the Self... the Soul, on the other hand, subtly signals the inner bodies and softly steers the personalized *aham* to self-emptiness.

Never, however, does SPIRIT seek to strong-arm the Self, nor does the Soul seek to excessively sway the *aham,* (and its kayas), by means of sinewy inspiration, or by steely imposition.

The disciplined disciple ardently delves into the all of daily doing, being always duty-discriminative, on direct account of his deliberately donning the divine diadem of Dharma.

The stalwart sadhaka espouses not the lesser stillness of the subdued *sukshama* senses; he selectively and covertly chooses to coalesce his essence with the superior stillness of the *Shunyata* SELF.

(The SHUNYATA SELF is the Strength and Synthesis of the SOUL's *nish-karma* service, tenderly tended toward the all of Existence.)

The disciplined disciple deems it randomly ridiculous not to 'willingly wonder' at just about everything *being* just naturally, Absolutely Awesome.

From out of the Absolute Spaciousness of SHUNYATA, the Dharmakaya as the sempiternal Self is synthetically stratified by SPIRIT, and is then purposefully sent out upon the very mysterious mission of taking on a seemingly objectified existence, as man.

The stalwart sadhaka consciously takes up the occult Challenge of CREATION and peregrinates the planet as a spiritually-polarized, highly-explorative, glamour-busting, darkness-scattering, grace-spreading and wisdom-mirroring, contractedly-downcast but constantly-content, Sacred Pilgrim of his ETERNAL SELF'S PURPOSE.

The disciplined disciple desires not to be adored, nor loved, for he knows without a shadow of a doubt that he is All of That, and much *More*.

The disciple wholeheartedly desires to demonstrate the Server's discipline of rendering Divine Aid and Loving Compassion, to all sentient beings.

This he endeavors to accomplish with an ardent devotion for the vital 'World Work' to be already-now *lovingly* activated upon the planet Earth… which presently houses Humanity's ongoing play of the 'Passionate Masquerade'.

The stalwart sadhaka seeks not to be accepted by God, for he knows that his Soul can never be rejected.

He sets his Heart rather, upon the setting of the world afire with Love for HIM, even as he dispassionately manducates on his planetary pudding.

The disciplined disciple has long ago, let go of the deceptive sedative of security; he has long ago, rid himself of the delusion of definiteness and dependability; he has long ago, discharged himself of the weighty dross of earthly demonstrability and validity; he has long ago, discovered that his distinctive dilemma was the indeterminableness of the Unknown, and (that) his driven decision and discerning direction, was the indubitableness of Divine Wisdom.

The stalwart sadhaka incessantly strives with all of his strength to secure the best possible chord of consciousness, which he should strike in tendering a true *service* to humankind... being firstly and fundamentally, the awakened *awareness* of his Absolute Absence and empty Self-Recognition.

The disciplined disciple deems to adopt the Tranquil Mind however much he undertakes and does; he deems to uphold the Tranquil Heart however much he emotes and feels; he deems to demonstrate the Tranquil Tongue however much he utters and talks; and he deems to decree the Tranquil Smile, all along the many magnetic miles of his Radiant Life.

The stalwart sadhaka does not interest himself in the sayings of a man's speech.

He seeks instead, a sacred access to the recesses of a man's Silence.

The disciplined disciple discusses little, discourses less, and discloses nothing.

(Yet upon his golden face shines openly the Light of all he Hides.)

The stalwart sadhaka sagaciously slices up SILENCE into seven Impersonal parts of Imperfect Pulchritude.

(And his personality pops-up pleasantly surprised with a yummy seven-piece, pecan pie of personalized Truth.)

The disciplined disciple has distinctly discerned that the more a man normally speaks, the less he is embedded in Truth or enfolded by Silence; and the more (that) the tongue prattles and talks, the more then, that the mind meanders and is lost.

Four Associative Aphorisms: "Big talk, bad Silence."

"Twisted talk, crooked Truth."

"Bold talk, shy Self."

"Sparse talk, essential Emptiness, (in view)."

The stalwart sadhaka seeks not the Self, nor the Not-Self, but only the ONE Breath where Absolute Being breathes.

He seeks not the Solitude where no other exists, but only the ABSOLUTE ALONENESS, wherein everyone Lives.

The disciplined disciple will demonstrate the kind of self-understanding which demands from his ongoing sadhana a detailed discernment of any delitescent degree of Divine *unreadiness*.

Divine unreadiness for example, may resemble the nature of a clandestine, delinquent dissension taken up against the undergoing of any further discipline as applied to an abstract attainment, such as the deepening of Divine *dhyana*.

Or perhaps, it could take on the innocent form of a seemingly harmless diversion, such as that, which a wandering *leela* may awaken.

Or perhaps, it may just reveal itself suddenly, in a surprised disclosure of an extremely subtle state of spiritualized *self-will*.

Or, mayhaps, it could even don the mask of the slightest form of lukewarmness at a most critical time in the sadhaka's spiritual development, thereby divulging a most delicate *deviation* away from the Divine.

The disciplined disciple is a student who is ever on the lookout for any retardative condition to the process of his Self-Awakening; he is that sincere seeker and serious pupil who will, with a detached admonishment readily admit to any leaning toward the least Divine deviation.

The disciplined disciple is that sadhaka who will always press onwards, and will persevere patiently vis-à-vis the paradoxical, (and often punishing), Spiritual Process of his eventual metamorphosis into the EMPTY-SELF... under the auspicious encouragement, unconditional Love and complete forgiveness of the Holy Mother's compassionate gaze.

* A Paradox for the Road

The stalwart sadhaka sings the song of an Empty Self slung across the skydome of his Destiny... whatever happens, *happens*; and whatsoever takes place, *takes place*; and my-Self is Itself a mere illusionary happening in time and space; and I Am Happy, and I have no desire that things should have been different; and I bear no judgment, for I Am the sole Judge of my whole world; and I Am the God that GOD full of Wonder, Awakened.

Glossary

Adi Shiva: Primal Shiva, third member of the Hindu Trinity known as the Lord of Destruction.

Aham: The subjective sense of "I am"; the "I exist".

Ahamkara: "I" as the always conditional ego; the pride of existence; egoism; vanity.

Ahimsa: The principle of non-violence; harmlessness; the five restraints and five moral observances.

Ananda: Bliss from the heart, Joy from the mind, Ecstasy from the body… all identifying with the Self.

Ashram: (from the sanskrit word "Shrama", *effort*); a center for spiritual studies and meditation, usually under the guidance of an Instructor, a Master or Guru.

Atma: The Divine Soul.

Atman: The Transcendental Self.

Avatar: A physical incarnation of the Divine Consciousness.

Baba-ji: The planet earth's "Mahavatar", (Great Avatar); deathless, he physically lives in the Himalayas, but His Omni-Presence bestows a guidance and constant blessing on the world, (and world events).

Baraka (Barakat): A blessing, grace, or gift of definite Divine benediction coming from a place, object, or person of holiness.

Bodhi: The state of Awakening or Illumination (leading to Liberation).

Bodhi Tree: The sacred tree under which the Buddha awakened and was Enlightened.

Bodhichitta: The Awakened mind; the mind of Enlightenment which manifests in compassion.

Bodhisattva: A Realized Buddha who has made a vow of service to all sentient beings, sacrificing his own immediate and complete liberation, to compassionately aid and uplift mankind.

Brahman: The Ultimate Reality; the Absolute; the Transcendental Self.

Budh: Budh or Buddh, being the root syllable for Bodhi, meaning 'awake'; therefore, by implication, the 'Awakened One', and thusly, a Buddha.

Buddhi: The Wisdom faculty; Higher Mind; Soul-ar Intuition; Pure Reason; Gnosis.

Chaitanya: Bhakti, Devotional Bliss; Ecstatic Consciousness; Great Bengali (Vaishnava) Saint of the 15-16th century, whose devotional passion for Krishna became legend.

Chenrezi: "Looking with clear eyes"; the Tibetan form of Avalokiteshvara, the Bodhisattva of Compassion.

Da: "The One Who Gives"; the Divine Giver of Inherent Heart, (or Love) Bliss.

Dadi: The God Giver of Grace; the Servant of Self and the Slave of Spirit; the dynamic *Father Principle* and gentle *Feminine Force* joined in Name.

Dharma: Divine Duty; daily right action; the Way (of Truth); Law of the Spirit.

Dharmakaya: Doctrine of the teachings of Buddha; the true nature of the Buddha which is identical with Absolute Reality; the essence of the universe; the transcendental space of Being.

Dharmata: The innate nature of Dharma, the fundamental Essence that is the clear basis of everything.

Diksha: Initiation; the transmission of wisdom (jnana), and the transfer of power (shakti), from Master to disciple.

Dokhma: A pit surrounded by a low stone tower with a grated top on which the Parsees place their dead.

Dhyana: Meditation or contemplation; the state of deep Stillness and inner Poise reached in advanced stages of meditation.

Green Tara: Embodies the 'active compassion' aspect of all Buddhas; the female Buddha of enlightened activity; she is said to have emanated from the tears of the left eye of Bodhisattva AVALOKETISHWARA, in order to aid Him in his great Compassionate Work; she also helps to remove obstacles and serves as a potent protector of her devotees.

Guru: Spiritual Teacher/Preceptor/Instructor/Guide/Master; one who is mature, ripe, or "heavy with the fruit" of Wisdom.

Hanuman: Hindu divinity representing the perfect disciple, who manifested in the form of a monkey; the devoted servant of Rama, his Lord.

Hara: A name for Shiva, representing the fire/heat of disintegration and destruction; the dispeller of darkness and ignorance.

Hari: The 'consoler'/'comforter'; the Divine Robber who removes, or steals, from the heart of his devotee, the negative conditions related to ignorance, sin and sorrow; one of the many forms of Vishnu.

Hridaya(m): The True Heart; the Heart of Hearts; the Cave of the Heart.

Hum: A sacred mantric syllable representing/facilitating the wisdom Mind of the Buddhas.

Indra: The Lord of the heavens; Hindu God of thunder/lightning symbolizing spiritual power and the flash, (or flashes), of Illumination.

Ishwara (Ishvara): Creator of the universe; the personification of the Absolute; Lord of the Manifest; the 'Lord' within man; a personalized, venerated form of the Lord.

Japa: A constant and rapid repetition of the Lord's name; the practice of mantra.

Ji: An adjunctive syllable given to a name as a sign of honoring and respect.

Jivatma: The incarnated Soul; the individualized, human Soul.

Jnana-Marg: The Path of Knowledge; the Way of Wisdom.

Kama: The Creative Principle; the Primal Impulse behind the desire of Existence to exist; also, often used in relation to passion, affection and (all the delights of) desire.

Karma: Law of cause and effect; action and reaction; 'as you sow, so shall you reap'.

Kaya(s): Body or vehicle of manifestation; various dimensions and manifestations of an enlightened being.

Krishna: An avatar who lived in India three millenniums before the Christian era and whose divine counsel to Arjuna, (who symbolizes the incarnated Soul), in the Bhagavad Gita, is revered by countless God-seekers; the Indian counterpart to Christ (Consciousness).

Krupa: Divine Grace emanating from the Guru.

Kwannon: Avalokiteshvara, Mahakaruna Buddha, the Buddha of Great Compassion; also known in Japan as Kannon or Kanzeon, in China as Kuan Yin, and in Tibet as Chenrezi.

Leela, (or Lila): A divine play, or action of the Lord vis-à-vis His Creation.

Linga(m): The male mark, sign, or symbol of Shiva; it represents the Fundamental Form, Primordial Power, or Pure Consciousness which cannot be destroyed by death, or by any other means; it also stands for the undying subtle body, the indivisible Monad, and Divinity Unclothed.

Lokesvara: A four-armed manifestation of Avalokiteshwara, the Bodhisattva of Compassion.

Mahakali: The Great Kali, a form of Shakti, as the embodiment of the Force of Destruction; also as Divine Wisdom which puts an end to all illusion; the Black One, the slayer of demons and the unreal.

Mahanam: The practice of the recitation of the Name of God; chanting the Great Name of the Supreme Lord.

Mahatma: A great Soul/Self in selfless service to the greater enlightenment of Humanity.

Mandir: Literally "abode of God"; home of a Deity; a temple honoring a Divinity, or housing the Divine.

Manjushri: Bodhisattva of Great Wisdom; in Tibetan Buddhism Manjushri embodies the incisive wisdom that dispels the darkness of ignorance.

Manna: Grace from heaven; the descent of Divine inspiration; a form of spiritual food giving self a sense of empowerment.

Mantra(m): Potent recitations, incantations and invocations made-up of sanskrit seed syllables and the names of Lords.

Mara: The incarnation of the Negative Force in Buddhism; it also symbolizes the desires and passions which enslave man, as well as those obstacles which may impede his progress towards enlightenment.

Maya: Illusion; relative phantom-existence; the created universe as being a play of illusion, and giving rise to false knowledge, untruth, and ignorance; the Veil which hides the Vision (of Truth).

Metanoia: A radical reorientation of the self being repolarized to the Self; a profound inner movement and repositioning of one's whole being through the surrender or relinquishment of the ego's normal hold on existence; a metamorphic modification, a transformative turnabout, or a total transfiguration.

Monad: The indivisible primordial Self; Spirit Essence; the Divine Womb or Primordial Matrix giving birth to a collectivity of Souls.

Muni: The science of abiding in inner Silence; an ascetic whose sadhana is Silence.

Nabhikalpa, Navikalpa Samadhi: A state of perfect samadhi; *absolute* tranquil abiding at the Center of the Self, where eventually, the seeds of all previous samskaras, (subconscious patterns, or vibrational impressions), are completely burnt, or neutralized.

Nadis: A network of subtle or energy channels of which the etheric body is composed.

Nirvana: A state of High Enlightenment, where true Liberation is released and Integral Oneness lived.

Glossary

Nish-Karma (Naishkarmya Karman): Similar to Wei Wu Wei... that is, *actionless action, effortless effort*; therefore, action, thought or emotion which has no karmic repercussions.

Om: The Spiritual sound of Creation; the Word (gone forth); the Verb; the Primordial Vibration which sustains all worlds.

Om Mani Padme Hum: lit. 'Om, Jewel in the Lotus (of the Heart), Hum'; a well known mantra in Tibetan Buddhism; the compassion mantra associated with Avalokiteshwara.

Om Tat Sat: "I Am the Truth which Is the very Essence of Om"; "I Am That".

Padmakara: 'Lotus Born', a synonym for Padmasambhava, or Guru Rinpoche.

Padmapani: Known as the "Lotus-Bearer"; one of the more common epithets of Avalokiteshvara, the Bodhisattva of Infinite Compassion.

Para Param Purusha: The Supreme High Lord; the Highest of the High; the God of Gods.

Prajna: Knowledge qualified by the Highest Consciousness; Universal-type Wisdom.

Prajnaparamita: The Goddess of transcendental wisdom; the wisdom of all buddhas personified in the enlightened form of a female deity. The *Prajnaparamita-Sutra* is regarded as the holy mother that feeds the bodhisattva with the amrita (nectar) of prajna (transcendental wisdom), and guides him to *paramita* (the other shore).

Pranaam: Profound salutation and humble obeisance.

Prarabdha (Pralabdha): The inevitable, present life destiny which is in accordance with our past karma; and whose influence, in the best of possible worlds, should be met with an open consciousness, and worked through.

Prasad: A blessed or divine gift; often refers to food that has been offered to God, and is thus blessed by Him through the intercession of a Guru, Saint, Priest or Holy Person.

Prashchit: True repentance as part of the process of Purification.

Prema: Love of God; Love of Self; and Divine Love for all of creation.

Puja: Ritual worship in which a deity is invoked in the form of an idol, or picture, and is propitiated as a Divine guest with offerings of flowers, fruits and other eatables, along with the recitation of appropriate mantras and an expression of relevant signs.

Purusha: The Primordial Lord; the Animating, or Primeval Male Principle in man; the "Creative Collectivity" of Creation; the Creative Cognized Self as Pure Spirit (male), as distinguished from Prakiti (feminine creative energy, matter, maya).

Pu'Tai (Bu'Tai), Ch'i-tzu: A wandering, wonder-working, miracle-making monk said to have lived in 10th century China; in all Chinese monasteries he is represented as the laughing Buddha; he was a lover and creator of many *paradoxes* of Ch'an, (or Zen), Buddhism; only at the time of his death did he reveal his true identity as an incarnation of the future Buddha MAITREYA.

Rama: The seventh Avatar, an incarnation of Vishnu and the hero of the Ramayana.

Roshi: In Zen, the venerable Master.

Sabhikalpa, Savikalpa Samadhi: A state of *temporary*, Spiritual Stillness and Absorption, in which the seeds of previous karma continue to exist.

Sadhak(a): Spiritual aspirant/student; a disciple; a shishya; a chela.

Sadhana : Spiritual discipline and practice; the duties of Discipleship.

Saddhu, Sadh: A wandering spiritual mendicant; a holy man, a saint; one who has attained siddhis (powers), through asceticism and intensely sustained effort.

Saiemoud : A sacred appellation of God; GOD, the Absolute; the LIFE of the Central Sun.

Samantabhadra: "He Who Is All-Pervading and All-Good", or "He Whose Beneficent Goodness Is Everywhere"; also known as Vajradhara; the ultimate Primordial Buddha, or Adi Buddha; one of the most significant Buddhas of Mahayana Buddhism and Dzogchen.

Samayas: Vows of engagement taken towards the Master and his lineage; a sacred pledge to follow the Dharma and uphold the spiritual path.

Samboghakaya: One of the three bodies of the Buddha; the body of Bliss or the enjoyment body; 'timeless ecstatic communication', without beginning or without end.

Samsara: The wheel of rebirth, the process of worldly life; the cycle of rebirths that a being goes through within the various modes of existence until final liberation is attained.

Sangha: A Buddhist community or brotherhood; in common usage, a confrererie or comradeship of similar Souls upon a spiritual Path.

Saraswati: The Hindu Mother Goddess embodying the *creative spirit* of all fine arts; She is the active Essence, or Consort of Brahma.

Sat Chit Ananda: Existence, Knowledge, Bliss.

Satguru: A spiritual Teacher of Truth.

Satsang, Sat-sangha: A meeting of devotees; "the company of Truth"; being associated with the presence of Sadhs, (Sadhus), Siddhas (perfected Adepts), and Self-Realized Masters.

Sensei: Honorable Teacher; Venerable Instructor.

Shakti: Universal energy of the active Feminine Principle; the Creative Power of the Manifest.

Sheik, Shaikh: The Master, or Chief Instructor, or Superior Guide of an order of Sufi dervishes.

Shiva: Third member of the Hindu Trinity known as the Lord of Destruction; however, He is also known as the Lord of the Totality of All-Being.

Shunyata: Emptiness, Nothingness; Silence; the ultimate Reality as Void, or Voidness.

Siddhi(s): Psychic powers attained through intense training and ascetic discipline.

Sishya: Pupil, disciple of a Murshid, or Pir (Sufi Master).

Sita: *("Furrow")* In early India, she was known as a fertility, or agricultural (Corn) Goddess, since the repositories of seed known as *furrows* were regarded as the earth's regenerative organs. As the wife of Rama, she is the very essence or light of femininity, the gem of womenhood and the jewel of virtue; she stands to His right, and is strongly devoted to Him; she symbolizes spousal loyalty, fidelity and love; and is the "substantial Shadow", and perfect reflective Light, of Rama.

Spanda: The Primal Pulse, or Pulsation of Creation; the Heartbeat of the Universe; the throbbing Beatific Bliss of Existence.

Subramanya, Skanda, Karttikeya, Murugan: The name of Shiva-Parvati's youngest son; handsome and powerful, he is brother to Ganesha, and holds the position of Supreme Commander of the Army of the Gods; his consorts are Devasena and Valli.

Suksham, Sukshama(s): The various vahanas, or vehicles of expression, surrounding the Soul; for example, the etheric envelope, the astral body, the causal casing, etcetera.

Sushumna: the central main energy channel located along the spinal column; it connects the base chakra to the Brahmarandhra at the top of the head; associated with the upliftment of the fiery essence.

Swaha, Svaha: A ritual bowing and honoring often accompanied by prayer, or invocation, following each offering, during sacrificial ceremonies, such as ritual fire practices.

Tamas: Quality of passivity, inertia, darkness.

Tapasya: Purification through sacrifice, penance, and self-discipline.

Tara: A popular deity in Tibetan Buddhism, said to have issued from the tears of Avalokiteshvara in order to help him in his Task; she embodies the feminine aspect of Compassion.

Tat Tvam Asi: 'That Thou Art God'; that is, God, or the Infinite.

Tyaga: Sacrifice, renunciation; and the eventual, disciplined dropping of all form-related predilections.

Vishnu: Lord of the Universe, Second Lord Creator, and Generator of All; Lord of Sacred Wisdom, Lord of Water, Lord Maintainer, the All-Pervader. The second Divinity in the Hindu Trinity whose role is to preserve and aid in the evolution of mankind.

Wali: A wandering Sufi saint.

White Tara: Born from the tears of Avalokiteshvara, the Buddha of Compassion; she grants long life; her three facial eyes represent the three doors to liberation (the three emptinesses) and the other four on her palms and soles symbolize the four immeasurables (love, compassion, joy and equanimity).

Woden: A later Germanic form of Odin, (Norse); with his constant thirst for Knowledge he became the wisest of Deities; he is also known as the mightiest of the warrior gods; blue-cloaked, he wears a wide-brimmed hat and carries with him a magic spear (his warrior-wizard aspect); he corresponds to Jupiter and to Zeus, his Roman and Greek counterparts.

Wyrd, Urdh: Teutonic Goddess of Destiny; Chief of the Norns whose Divine task lies in directing the winds of Destiny, in regard to both mortals and gods.

Yama: The God/Ruler of Death in the Vedas.

Yamantaka: a Mahayana Buddhist deity; one of the eight Dharmapalas, Protectors of the Teaching of the Buddhas; 'Yama' is the name of the god of death, and 'Antaka' means 'terminator'...'the terminator or defeater of death'.

Yogi: One who practices yoga and undertakes its disciplines out of desire for Yog, (Union).

Yoni: The feminine, receptive principle; the female sexual organ; the original Creative Source; the doorway of Spirit descending into the manifest world.

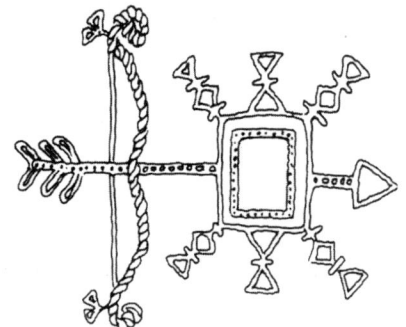

Orange Palm and Magnificent Magus Publications Inc.©
235 René Lévesque Boulevard East, Suite 310
Montréal, Québec, H2X 1N8, Canada
Telephone: (514) 255-8700
Facsimile: (514) 255-0478
E-mail: info@palmpublications.com
Web site: http://www.palmpublications.com